Praise for Rescued Volume 1

"The stories of these 12 rescue cats are inspiring and moving, and hearing them through the cats' own perspective is a particularly interesting experience. I know Henri would approve."
— Will Braden, Creator of *Henri, le Chat Noir*

"By approaching these stories from the perspective of the cats, *Rescued* reveals the nuances of cat rescue that will make you revisit your own experiences in a new light."
— Kate Benjamin, catification expert and founder of Hauspanther LLC

"Be prepared to giggle, gasp a bit and definitely applaud these fine felines who teach us the value of being kind, being candid and living in the me-NOW."
— Arden Moore, founder of FourLeggedLife.com and Casey the Pet Safety Cat

"Even though the twelve stories are all different, they are also universal stories of compassion, caring and love. As you meet the cats, you will, no doubt, think about your own rescue cat's story. This book is both a tribute to the resilience of rescue cats and a love letter to these special cats."
— Ingrid King, award winning author and publisher/founder of The Conscious Cat, consciouscat.net

Rescued Volume 2

Rescued Volume 2
The Healing Stories of 12 Cats, Through Their Eyes

Edited by Janiss Garza

FitCat Publishing
Los Angeles

Copyright ©2017 FitCat Enterprises, Inc.

Published by:
FitCat Publishing
P.O. Box 411461
Los Angeles, CA 90041
www.fitcatinc.com

All rights reserved. No part of this book may be used or reproduced in any manner without written permission except in the case of reprints in the context of reviews.

Publisher's Cataloging-In-Publication Data
(Prepared by The Donohue Group, Inc.)

Names: Garza, Janiss, editor.
Title: Rescued. Volume 2, The healing stories of 12 cats, through their eyes / edited by Janiss Garza.
Other Titles: Healing stories of 12 cats, through their eyes
Description: Los Angeles : FitCat Publishing, [2017]
Identifiers: LCCN 2016915870 | ISBN 978-1-941433-04-1 | ISBN 978-1-941433-05-8 (ebook)
Subjects: LCSH: Cat rescue--Anecdotes. | Cats--Health--Anecdotes. | Cat owners--Psychology--Anecdotes. | Human-animal relationships--Anecdotes.
Classification: LCC HV4743 .R47 2017 (print) | LCC HV4743 (ebook) | DDC 636.8/0832--dc23

Front cover photograph by Julie McAlee.
Back cover photograph by Karen Nichols.
All other photos used with authors' permission.
Cover design by Debbie Glovatsky, www.glogirlydesign.com.

Table of Contents

Foreword   ix
Zorro: The Ragdoll's Dance   1
Mad Maxine: Feline Road to Recovery   21
Allie: My Fair Kitten   35
Wu Kitty: Rescued From The Row   58
Belladonna: Sweet Sugar Kitty   78
The Story of Little Pip   96
The World According to Banzai   112
Pounce Takes a Chance   129
Ashton: A Scary Situation   145
Piggy: The Claw Machine Cat   161
Jazmine's Story...by Mr. Jazz   177
Sparky: It's Not Over Until the Cat Lady Sings   196
The Authors Behind the Cats   212
About the Editor   219

FOREWORD

I've always cheered for the underdog, the one who unexpectedly rises from the ashes to do great things, find love, or simply make it through to the other side of a difficult situation. I'm also an optimist who refuses to give up on others or myself. This is one of the reasons why I connected with *Rescued Volume 2: The Healing Stories of 12 Cats, Through Their Eyes*.

Another reason I connected with the book is because it reminds me of my mother. Mom has always been an inspiration and living model of someone who has not only rescued cats, but was the recipient of a feline's magical healing power.

When I was ten years old, I remember her bringing home a tiny abandoned kitten that had been hanging around the warehouse where she worked. She'd waited

Rescued Volume 2

until she knew the mother wouldn't return, and then brought home the tuxedo baby, who we named "Bobbi." It was 1980, and Mom didn't know much about taking care of an unweaned kitten, but her maternal skills kicked in. She fed Bobbi with a bottle dropper and kept her safe from the other cats inside a warm, blanket-filled hamster cage. During the day, she took the kitten to work with her, letting her snooze inside the pouch of her flannel shirt's pocket. Bobbi grew to be strong and healthy, and of course, she and Mom had a lasting bond.

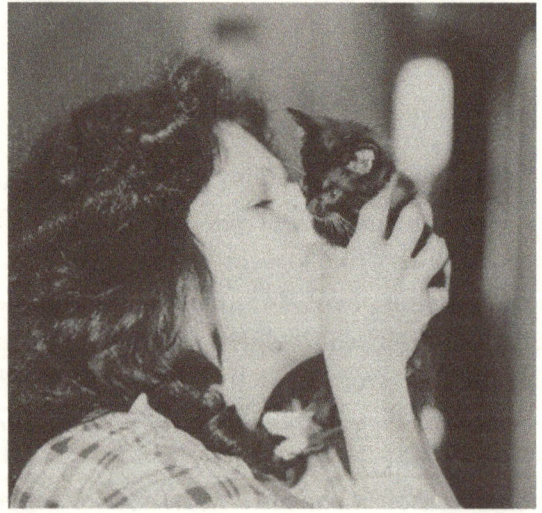

Later in her life, Mom would experience yet another significant relationship with a feline. Spooker, who Bobbi birthed before she'd been spayed, was the kitten Mom kept from the litter. Like his mama, he was a tuxedo, but grew to be twice her petite size. The only way to describe Mom and Spooker's 14-year relationship was "best friends." He stuck by her side through a bad

Foreword

marriage, emotional upheaval, and multiple moves between Florida and Minnesota. He never complained. Mom has often said she doesn't know if she could have made it through without Spooker. He was the medicine and therapy she needed to move through a dark tunnel and make it to the other side.

My mother's stories aren't unique by any means. Every day there are humans and cats supporting and healing one another. There's love and kindness that rescues and unconditionally loves the underdogs of this world. In a time when so much bad news blankets the media, these are the stories that keep me going. These are the tales that inspire us to be better people. Janiss Garza has assembled a collection of stories by passionate authors who've lived through this kind of special love with cats. *Rescued Volume 2: The Healing Stories of 12 Cats, Through Their Eyes* reminds us of life's goodness, and reassures us that resurrection and healing are happening around us all the time...for humans and cats alike.

Angie Bailey, author
Texts from Mittens
whiskerslist: the kitty classifieds
angie-bailey.com

ZORRO: THE RAGDOLL'S DANCE

Humans call us Floppy Cats. We're the Ragdoll and we dance with our bodies. The Ragdoll's dance is rooted in the depths of our psyche and tempted forth in a loving world. It exudes trust and joy, innocence and optimism. But when the Ragdoll's trust is broken, the dance gets buried deeply.

Dare we dance again in a dangerous world?

Frigid midafternoon temperatures promised an unbearable night. The sun was low on the flat gray horizon of the wooded boreal swamp. Bitter cold burrowed under my thick white fur, all the way down to my skin. It prickled along my tail, and the ice on the road bit deep into my paw

Rescued Volume 2

pads. A wolf howled nearby, hidden by the thick tangle of spruce and tamarack. Ancient survival instincts kicked in, and I moved cautiously and quickly. Me, who'd never been outside in my life. My world had turned upside down in one terrible moment.

I had to find shelter. I resisted the urge to dart into the woods, which offered cover but also housed animals that would eat me. I crept along the side of an icy dirt road, knowing not to venture too far into the ditch, which was now filled with snow. A Ragdoll has big paws, but those paws won't keep you from sinking. I needed to preserve my warmth and energy.

I was no Ragdoll at this moment, only a scared anycat, relying on instinct and teetering on survival, accessing primal impulses to stay alive.

A day ago? A moment ago? I could not forget hitting the icy ground hard on my side, the car door slamming, nostrils overpowered with the smell of fumes as the engine shrieked and the car sped away. My blue eyes were wide with fright, my ears pinned close to my head, and I began to shiver, the cold overtaking me.

At that moment, I left all trust behind.

No more loose and easy body. Ragdolls flop — it is our dance. I would not allow that now. Every footfall was driven with fear and survival.

Through the brushy alder on the side of the road, I glimpsed the warm lights of a human's home. Cautiously, I crept down the driveway, but it was too cold for anyone to be out and about. The light came from the house, but an attached garage was dark and the large garage door was open. Picking up speed to avoid being

Zorro: The Ragdoll's Dance

noticed, I ran for the garage, scurrying along one side wall, as far from the parked cars as possible. I pressed against the back wall, squeezing behind plywood pieces that leaned over me. Trembling, I stayed there for hours, even when I heard one of the humans come out and do something that made that big door close.

🐾 🐾 🐾

"There's a cat in the garage!"
Busted!
I dashed for my hiding place. I'd not let my guard down again, that was for sure. I'd been hunting. Birds sometimes flew into the garage and hopped around on the floor. I was hungry, but in no hurry to venture outside, even though the humans often had the garage door open. It was cold in the garage, but protected from the bitter winds that blew in from the woods and the north.

"Chris! There's a beautiful cat in the garage."
Beautiful! I *am* a Ragdoll. But I hadn't thought about beauty lately, just about surviving. My fur was dirty and matted. Beauty was for a cultured world, with warm houses like the place I used to live. My heart squeezed in a bitter way and I pushed the thought of those people and that warm house out of my mind.

I must survive.
"Chris, come out here."
They weren't getting anywhere near me. I would be no one's cat again. I pressed against the cold wall in my familiar hiding place. My stomach rumbled. I'd only successfully caught one bird in the garage.

Rescued Volume 2

The woman continued to chatter. "He's hiding now. I think it's a boy. He's huge. White and black and fluffy. Oh, Chris, he's going to die out here!"

Die? That was the last thing on my mind. I was going to survive, even if I had to kill a hundred birds to do it. And those people would never see me again, if they could help it.

But the humans didn't give up. They put out food and water in the garage. The woman had to break and refill the water several times a day because it kept freezing. And she worried about my warmth. I certainly could have been more comfortable, but I was doing okay out of the cold.

The humans began closing the garage door at night to keep the cold air out. They struggled with this decision, too. Humans make things so hard. They talked about another "feral" who'd lived in the garage, one bitter winter. They had named him "Two Day" because he came around every few days. But the humans shut

Zorro: The Ragdoll's Dance

the garage door one cold night, after Two Day had gone into the garage, and that cat got so annoyed that he left the next day and never came back.

Me, I know a meal when I see one.

The humans quickly got used to the fact that I was okay with them shutting the garage door at night. They even made me a bed of sorts. They threw some straw in a large rubber tub. I loved it. Then, as humans do, they overthought the situation and tried to make me a better shelter.

"Zorro," the woman called. I would not let her see me. They'd at least had the sense to put that straw bed way back in the garage where I could hide.

"Zorro! I made you a better shelter."

She was trying to get me used to the sound of her voice, because she talked to me now, every time she came out into the garage. And "Zorro"? They liked the markings on my face that looked like a mask.

"I made this from a plastic tote. It has a cover, and dry straw, and an entrance."

I checked it out but I didn't use it. It made me feel trapped and it didn't have an exit door. What if some fierce animal cornered me in that "feral shelter," as she called it? I was perfectly happy in my straw bed. The humans finally got the idea. They added a litter box, which I started to use. Thankfully, I could finally bury my business instead of leaving it exposed.

The winter dragged on, but the cold air didn't bother me as long as I had cover. On windless, sunny days,

Rescued Volume 2

I sat outside, amazing the humans with my ability to endure what they called "sub-zero temps." They'd sit at a table inside the house and watch me through their window. It felt good to be getting their interest, at a safe distance. I fixed them with a smoldering look and held up a paw, just to be cute. My paws would dance, even if my body didn't.

The humans didn't want me sitting in the cold snow. The concrete floor of the garage was cold, too. They filled an old plastic sled with dry straw and put it toward the front of the garage so I could get sun during the day. Then they added a pad on top of the straw. The pad was warm and had soft fabric covering it.

My purr is soft and barely audible, but it rumbled through my body the first time I stepped onto that pad, and contentment radiated through my body. I spent many happy hours on my warm pad, atop a bed of straw. I was well fed now and didn't have to worry about catching birds. The humans continued to watch me through the window and the woman talked to me each time she came into the garage. I stopped running and hiding and would sit in my sled, watching her. She could look at me and talk, but if she got too close, I would disappear. She figured out the magic barrier pretty quickly, and let me relax on my sled bed.

🐾 🐾 🐾

A shift in the air, a slight hint of warmth grew over the days. The sun inched higher and it was possible to sit in its yellow beams for longer periods of time.

Zorro: The Ragdoll's Dance

I was not lured by the green conifers of the nearby woods. I could smell and hear the wolves and the foxes waiting in the darkness. Better to stay in the garage, or in the yard, close to the house. I even began to see patches of grass through the snow, which was quickly receding and glistening with new moisture. Change was afoot. The humans scurried about. I'd heard talk of a "move" but I wasn't sure what that meant. Would they stay here and feed me? What was going to be moved?

"I can't leave him here. I could never live with myself!"
"But you have to catch him."
"I'll find a trap."

Trap!

I hid in the garage more, even though the sun tempted me outside. The humans forged along with more urgency now. They hauled empty boxes into their house, filled the boxes, and stacked them out in the garage. There were all kinds of smells in those boxes. Old books. The ashes of departed cats. The crystal clear smell of wine glasses, wrapped carefully and smudged with the inky smell of news print. Old clothes, folded and full of the scent of these humans, and of other cats who lived in this house. Some of the boxes were hauled away, but most remained in the garage, waiting for something. "The move."

I knew one thing for sure. No one was going to trap *me*. I'd never dance again, and I'd never set paw in a trap.

🐾 🐾 🐾

Rescued Volume 2

The man pulled into the garage one day and lifted the trap out of his car; a clattery, rusty contraption with a door that banged against it. It was big enough to hold three of me. I watched him from my hiding place in the garage, eyes narrowed. A low growl grew deep in my throat. Things were working so well. I got fed. I got to sprawl in the sun on my heating pad. I got to hide when I wanted. I'd even begun singing, in the lusty way that toms sing for a female. Why bring this ugly contraption into the picture?

The boxes continued to pile up in the garage, forcing the humans to park their cars outside. I climbed on the boxes at night, and hid behind them during the day if the humans got too close. I wouldn't even lift a paw now, not even give those humans a smoldering look through their window, not even make them smile. I hid more, and this had the woman worried—I could hear it in her voice.

"We only have a few weeks! What if we can't get him?"

"*What if?*" What did that mean?

"It's warm enough now. Put something tempting in the trap."

And so it started. They'd been feeding me dry food all winter. But they put tempting, soft food treats in the trap, toward the back. The weather was nice now, just about freezing, and the treats never froze, but kept sending their aroma my way. For fun once, in full view of the humans watching through their window as they ate lunch, I tapped the door of the trap with one big paw. The door came slamming done, the trap empty. I rubbed my face against the trap, taking my time, showing them

Zorro: The Ragdoll's Dance

who was boss. I saw their look of temporary defeat, but they only got more determined. Better and smellier treats went into the trap, and they created a little path of bits of treat leading up to the door. As if I were so brainless.

🐾 🐾 🐾

A huge *HISSS* jarred me out of slumber, and I jumped upright on all fours, staring into the intense glare of a large gray tabby. He had the musk of a male in search of a mate, and an otherworldly blur outlined his sleek and muscled frame. Light filtered through the garage and back to my hiding place, giving me just enough light to see him.

"Who are you?" I tried to sound male and grownup, but my voice came out more like a chirp.

He raised a great paw and smacked me across the face. An outraged yowl rose in my throat, but he cut me off. "I am Two Day! Get in the trap!" he screamed.

I trembled. Once, so long ago I'd almost forgotten, my mother told me of these cats, as I burrowed my head in her soft Ragdoll fur. They only come if you need them, she said. Visitors from the place where cats become greater, once passed on and no longer limited by this earth.

I quavered. He towered over me. It seemed he'd gotten bigger.

"I'll not go in a trap!" Surely to walk into a trap was beneath any cat's dignity. "You didn't." And as I spoke, I realized who he was. He was the feral who these humans

Rescued Volume 2

tried to rescue, the one who would not stay in the garage, who never came back after the garage door was closed with him inside on a cold winter night.

"There is no trap big enough to hold me," he snarled, and the sharp ivory curve of his front incisors glistened. His claws were so long that they were visible even retracted. "You, Ragdoll, are another matter."

Ragdoll! He said it like an insult!

"Ragdolls are fierce, too!" It came out more like a squeak than the roar I'd intended.

He regarded me with narrowed eyes. "Do you want to meet the same end as I did? Ripped apart by hungry wolves, howling at their victory? "It was my destiny to be wild. It is your destiny to dance."

Dance.

The old muscle memories, the lift of a paw, the tilt of a head, leading into a flop onto my side. My paws longed to start the dance. I'd done it with trusted humans once, who I thought loved me. They'd acted like they loved me, petted and fed me, until that day when things irretrievably turned and they flung me from a car onto the icy packed snow on a dirt road.

"You will dance again," the tom growled. "Do not turn from your calling. Go into the trap."

I wanted to dance. Every nerve in my body remembered those moves. The Ragdoll is wired to be happy, innocent, and alive with the dance. Dare I?

"You cannot dance out here when you have to worry about surviving. Don't you understand that, stupid youngster?" The tom smacked me again, and my face stung. He disappeared suddenly in a blaze of fiery light,

Zorro: The Ragdoll's Dance

my ears ringing with his insults, my body remembering the temptation of what I'd forced myself to forget — the Ragdoll's dance.

🐾 🐾 🐾

In the dark of night, the humans asleep and the lights off in the house, I stood in front of the trap and stared at it. The door hung open, a fresh and tasty treat toward the back. That blasted tom had found the secret to my heart. How I missed moving like a Ragdoll. We vibrate with it, we thrive with it, we cannot help it. And I'd suppressed it for so long.

The tuna in the back of the trap was in a small dish. Its salty and pungent odor made my mouth water and made me think of a dish once in a warm house with humans who I thought I trusted. A time when I willingly danced, flopped onto my side, and waved my paws.

Those same paws trembled, and the tart, salty smell of the tuna water pulled me closer. My face still smarted from the great tom's smack. How could one wish to be ripped to pieces in the woods, dying alone with the howls of bloodthirsty canines all around? I only wanted to dance again, feel the soft touch of a human's hand, flop on my side and back and wave my paws. Would I find that love again?

What a beautiful cat! Surely these people wouldn't turn on me. Surely they'd love me, not throw me out of a car. I could see the longing looks on their faces as we flirted through the window where they watched me. Surely there had to be humans that could be trusted!

Rescued Volume 2

I leapt with this thought before it could escape my head and my paws would betray me. I ran into the trap toward the tuna and gobbled it down, the triggered door slamming shut behind me.

🐾 🐾 🐾

The man came out first, in the dark. The clatter of the trap door had woken him up. The woman was right behind him.

"It worked." I could hear the relief in his voice. I could see the relief in the woman's face. But fear had taken over me again, the dance long forgotten. I hissed if they got too close, and I smacked the inside of the cage hard with a big paw. I knew how to sound fearsome. They backed off. The woman put a big towel over the cage so that I wouldn't have to see anything, and then, as daylight strengthened, she loaded me into her car.

Sometime later, we came to a stop. She opened the hatch of her car door, lifted the towel, and she and another woman peered at me.

"Beautiful!" said the other woman. "Yep, he's a male." She said something about unneutered males and their musky smell. "Neuter and vaccinate?" the woman in white asked.

The human nodded. I trembled in the cage, my eyes wide, and smacked at the inside of the trap again.

"We'll check for a microchip, too. Are you going to keep him?"

Keep me? Who gets to keep ME?

Zorro: The Ragdoll's Dance

The woman nodded and shrugged her shoulders at the same time. "I hope so. Depends upon if I can tame him." *Tame me!*

"If not," she continued, "I have a friend with a farm that will take him. He could live in her barn. But I only have a week before we have to move." Again, the moving. What did it mean?

Back at the house, I looked longingly at the garage, now full of boxes. My sled bed sat, unused. The woman carried me in a plastic carrier, inside. She took me in a room with her and shut the door.

She was still smart enough not to get her hands too close to the cage. Even though I was groggy from the drugs at the veterinarian's, I was still mad and scared. The place between my hind legs ached and itched a little. I heard them tell my human that I had an amazing "pedal reflex." Apparently, my feet wanted to dance while I was completely asleep under their drugs. Well, what do you expect? I am a Ragdoll! Not a happy one at this moment, though.

The woman put a thick glove on her hand and reached toward the door of the plastic cat carrier where I sat. I lunged and spat and swatted at the door, but I never bared my claws or used teeth. I heard her take a deep breath, and then she unlatched the door and got her hand out of the way, quickly. I darted into a closet and hid, growling the entire time.

She should have kept me in the cage. Even though I growled and slammed at the door with my big paw,

Rescued Volume 2

at least I was beginning to feel safe. Now I was out in the open again. Not outside. The room was nice and warm. But still, hiding! What else could I do?

The woman realized, it, too.

She and the man would squeeze into the small room. I hid in the closet behind boxes and did not come out until they left. They talked in urgent voices about the silly things humans worry about.

"I'm screwed," she said. "How am I going to catch him?"

Too bad you didn't think of that, human. What choice did I have but to hide? My heart raced. I ate very little. I know they were worried. And the "move" date loomed. If they even came near the closet, I growled to tell them to stay away. Mostly, they obeyed. But there was a deadline coming. I was beginning to understand that they were going to leave this place, and they wanted to take me with them.

I was not sure how I felt about that.

Yes, I loved the memory of the woman talking to me in the garage. Why couldn't things have stayed that way? I was happy on my straw, in the sun, sleeping in the garage, even though it was cold. If not for that damned feral tom, Two Day, I would never have gone in the trap! Why did things have to change?

But change was coming, and quickly. The woman talked to a vet tech on the phone. That vet tech had rescued and tamed feral cats far wilder than me. And I guess that the tech had some good advice, because not long after, the woman soon appeared with a large cat carrier that a friend no longer needed.

I hid in the closet, and growled and hissed.

Zorro: The Ragdoll's Dance

"This is going to be your home for the next several days," she said. She talked to me, just like she did in the garage. Only this time, change and fear laced the air around us. "Now I just have to catch you."

I could feel the fear in her rise up. It seemed to fill the small room with heavy and chaotic uncertainty. How could I inspire such fear in a human?

"I've never done this before," she whispered to no one.

She took her time, hours perhaps, before finally forcing herself into motion. She would try to move and then stop. I could almost feel her mind, plotting the steps: *How can I catch you, Ragdoll cat?*

"I know you're just afraid," she whispered. "I know you're not really mean."

What was I? I no longer knew. A beautiful, once pampered cat who loved to dance. Who had been betrayed cruelly by one set of humans. Why should I believe these new humans would be any better?

Would I ever get to dance again, or would I spend my lifetime crouching in fear, hissing and swatting, hiding behind whatever I could find? I missed my dance, and it felt so far away.

"What do I do?" I whispered. Perhaps the Great Cat would hear me. But the glaring face of the gray tom suddenly loomed before me.

"Let her catch you," Two Day hissed. "Do you want to dance again, ever?"

He vanished and the woman began to move. She'd put on a heavy jacket, gloves on her hands, and some sort of helmet that covered her face. The big cat carrier stood behind her, door open.

Rescued Volume 2

Cautiously, she moved toward the boxes I was hiding behind, cornering me in the closet.

I hissed and spat.

I heard her gulp and breathe in slowly and deliberately. Then she lunged over the boxes, quickly grabbing me with those gloved hands. I struggled and twisted and hissed and spat as loudly as I could.

"Holy god, you're strong!" she yelled. Gasping and trying to hold on to the force of a muscular male Ragdoll, she stumbled toward the carrier and shoved me in, slamming the carrier door shut. She sat down and stared at me through the wire door of the cat carrier, breathing deeply, her eyes as wide as mine. Both of us were shaking, but not once had I bitten her, and I had not used my claws. I growled at her instead, a low and steady warning.

I remained in the cage inside the room, for several days. It contained a litter box, and food and water. At one point, I heard the woman explain to the man that the cage was supposed to give me a sense of security and be my temporary home. I did feel more secure in the enclosed space, and she had the sense to cover the cage with a towel again, to keep me from being frightened by stimuli around me.

But then, early one morning, the humans picked up the cage with me in it, and loaded it into a car with a panting dog next to me in another cage. A panting, huge, smelly dog! I could hardly hear myself think! Great Cat! I hoped I wouldn't be in this car for long.

Zorro: The Ragdoll's Dance

Then, from my cage, I watched the woman bring five cat carriers from her home and load them into the other car. Five cats! I knew there had been cats inside—I'd seen them staring at me through the windows, I'd smelled them on the humans' possessions, I'd screamed at them through the glass at night as the humans slept. Still...I'd not known how many were in the house. I could hear one of them complaining softly. The woman stuck her finger into that carrier and murmured something to the cat. Then, mercifully, she remembered me. She returned to our vehicle and draped a sheet over my carrier so at least I wouldn't have to see anything. But it couldn't block out the excited panting of the dog.

How would it feel to leave this place? Where were we going and was it permanent? I would miss my nice sled bed, with the warm pad. I wouldn't miss the cold, and the wolves I'd heard howling in the woods around the house. I wondered where we were going. The humans had talked about a place called Vermont. "Green Mountains," it means. But what did it mean for me?

The trip took three days! I know that the humans were going to try to do it in two days. But they stopped so often on the road to check on us all that the trip stretched into a longer journey. There was a shorter route, the woman said, that we couldn't take because one of the cats could not be vaccinated.

The woman sprayed something called Calming Essence in the cars, and it didn't bother me too much. She used Feliway spray, too. She fed the dog a relaxing soft chew and the dog seemed to settle down a bit, thank Cat. The woman had given me food and water but I had very little appetite. We stopped at motels both nights but it was warm enough outside that I could stay in the car. And actually, I was grateful for a break from the dog. The woman kept my cage covered so that I would hopefully relax. Strangely, I *was* feeling more relaxed. I had my safe space, and it was covered. The humans seemed to be relaxing, too, as we got closer to our destination.

After three days, we arrived. I knew this was the place because the woman and the man got out of the cars, hugged, and laughed. I heard tears in the woman's voice, as well.

The woman got me out of the car, took me into the new house, and isolated me in a room with food, water, and a litter box. She opened the cat carrier and I hunched in the back, growling softly. She left the room and shut the door. This room was bigger than the room I'd been kept in on the other side of this "move," but not as big as the garage. It was cool, but not cold. Cautiously, I checked out the space, located all the hiding places, and ate a bit of food. It tasted good after a few days of not eating much at all.

I could hear the humans, and the cats and dog, downstairs. But every chance she had, the woman came into my room. She worked on her laptop as I hid behind an old, shabby built-in bookcase. And she talked to me. Over the weeks, I found myself waiting and wanting to hear her voice.

Zorro: The Ragdoll's Dance

"Zorro," she said, softly. "Zorro, I can't wait for you to come out."

I growled behind the bookcase, but old feelings pulled at me. My paws began to tingle.

"Do it," hissed Two Day. I thought I saw him in the low light of this room, just beyond the bookcase.

I put a paw out slowly, growling the entire time. I peeked quietly around the corner, and the woman saw me.

Her eyes were warm, like my cat mother's eyes when I burrowed into her soft Ragdoll fur.

I backed quickly behind the bookcase, out of view, growling. But my paws twitched with old memories of the dance. I could remember, almost imagine, the pressure of my head, leaning into a soft human hand, totally releasing into a flop onto the floor, waving my paws in the air.

"Zorro," she whispered.

Zorro. Zorro. Zorro. Time expanded and contracted. She softly called my name over a period of days, weeks, longer. Slowly I crept, closer, closer, the dance singing inside me, daring me to again engage with a human, to trust.

Her fingers touched the side of my face.

I leaned into her hand, growling and purring at the same time. And then I felt my body, my paws, come alive. I flopped onto the floor. She knew better than to intrude and did not try to pet me or rub my belly. That would come later. The growl and the purr blended, and my paws danced, released of their fear. My paws flexed and waved their intentions to the air, to the wind, and the woman smiled. I thought I saw those human tears glisten on her cheeks. And so quietly that I might have been imagining it, I thought I heard a fierce gray tom whisper, "Dance, Ragdoll, dance! It is your destiny."

🐾 🐾 🐾

I don't growl now and I take as much attention as I can get from my humans. Every so often, caution and fear will overtake me if someone new comes into the house, or is a bit too forward. I am a handsome boy, and people are drawn to me. But I get past the fear quickly. I dance all day, every opportunity I get, leaning into a hand, rolling on my side, fixing the humans with a smoldering look as only a Ragdoll's blue eyes can do, waving my dancing paws.

Mad Maxine: Feline Road to Recovery

Yes I am judging you from the highest tier of my cat tree, no I am not coming down, and *of course* I expect you to indulge me post-haste with gentle scritches and loves. At this point I imagine you're having trouble deciding what to make of me. I am told first impressions are important, so hissing the first time I lay eyes on you is likely starting things off on the wrong foot. But there's the rub. I, Maxine of the Catmandu, have only three feet. All wrong. So you see, this is the only way I *can* kick things off.

Oh bother, now you're giving me that wary human look I am so keen to avoid. I don't require human pity. Can't you see I'm sitting a foot above your head? Pun, by the way, not intended. Nobody put me up here. I climbed this cat tree all on my own, thank you very much. I climb a lot of things, like the back of that chair you're standing next to. My bite is just as fierce as the next cat's, but humans rarely see that. Old, blind, deaf, or missing the usual number of parts doesn't make us defective. That is the kind of thinking that leaves a bad first impression, and the fault is not on us.

But I see you're still here. You could have veered left through the magnet-locked door to visit the four-legged cats, or backed up and gone next door to Kittenmandu, but here you are parked beneath my tree. So lift your hand and I'll start my motor, because this is my road to recovery.

The way Mother told it, my siblings and I were born on a back road in Topaz Lake during a mild December. *Mild* is not the word I'd use. My toe pads were so cold I felt like I was walking on marbles for the first few months of my life. At night my sisters and brothers would pile under a sage bush or discarded cardboard box and Mother would wash each of our heads and sing to us until we forgot about the savage cold.

March changed everything. One of my brothers disappeared first, then a sister. Days passed. We searched in groups. I suspected coyotes but I didn't voice my suspicions while the others still had hope. Mother's songs grew gnarled with grief. Instead of offering soft massages when I rested my head against her belly, she got up and slashed her claws through the bark of decaying trees. When Mother thought we were asleep, she snuck out in the dead of night to look for her lost children. One night she left and never came back.

Maxine: Feline Road to Recovery

By April it was just me. The temperature inched up to the fifties, drawing out more mice and birds. Unfortunately, the mice and birds weren't the only creatures the warmer weather courted. It's significantly more difficult to hunt without backup, especially when you have to avoid being hunted yourself. I lost count of how many meals my yowling stomach chased away. Felines are supposed to be expert huntresses. Oh, the *shame*.

One afternoon in the thick of my demoralization, I caught the downwind aroma of chicken. Nothing wild could smell heavenly enough to make me weak in the paws, so I assumed it was leftovers from tourist litter. I followed the smell to a metal box somewhat larger than my body and noticed a small paper plate inside with saucy chopped bits. Definitely tourist trash. I padded inside and made my way to the scraps. *Clang!* The box slammed behind me and I flipped and thrashed against the icy bars. No use — this wasn't trash, it was a trap. Maybe the very same one that stole the rest of my family. Were they dead? Was I next? All I could do was wait. I did not eat that night.

The drive to my next prison was hot and pothole laden. I could hear my captor talking in the driver's seat but thanks to the dim box I'd been unceremoniously stuffed into, I couldn't appraise my surroundings. The engine died and a moment later I heard a *click-whoosh*. I recalled the same sound the morning after my abduction when they loaded my cage into the back of my captor's vehicle.

Rescued Volume 2

Click.
Click.
Click.
Click.
"Hello? I'm here to drop off Maxine."
"Oh, welcome to Catmandu! I'm Linda."

This *Linda* seemed to be the new warden. Was my incarceration here meant to be longer than the one previous? Apparently my new cell designation was something called "Kitten Q." My box swished again and I slid against the side. More footsteps. More talking. More...happy felines? I pressed my ear to the box. There was a cacophony of voices in my native sandpaper tongue. The number of dialects was startling and yet, for the most part, they sounded casual, content even! What were they doing to these cats? Surely the poor fools had to be brainwashed. But I didn't get the opportunity to dwell on my theories because a rush of cold air swept down my spine and I realized my box was open. Two faces were staring down at me: the one who brought me here and a strawberry-blonde human female.

"Hello, Max," said Linda.

I hissed.

"She's very feral."

I turned at the voice of my old warden and flattened my ears to my head. Who were they calling feral? They catnapped me and now expected me to play *nice*?

"We'll work with her," Linda said reassuringly. "We have a lot of great volunteers. Hopefully we can socialize her and find her a forever home."

I *had* a forever home.

Maxine: Feline Road to Recovery

One good thing I can say about my first six weeks in Catmandu was the food was several steps above the meager prey and tourist trash I had been living on. Friskies was what they used to lure me into the trap at Topaz — I recognized the smell the first time they tried to serve me dinner. I resisted at first — you can hardly blame me, foul memories and all — but the feeding frenzies of my fellow inmates clued me in to what I was missing. The Friskies came twice a day, once in the morning and once in the evening. Between meals, several bowls of what I thought were colored pebbles sat around the facility. They were surprisingly edible.

Compared to my previous prison, Kitten Q was moderately sized. According to conversations I'd heard between Linda and her various human guests, the building used to be an old daycare center. She had rented it, cleaned it, and repurposed it as a "cat sanctuary." I took issue with the last part, but I digress. As a former daycare center, the room had plenty of high shelves that cats could use to climb and hide, plus other added amenities such as cat trees and chairs and boxes. I took full advantage of those boxes and shelves when the guards came in for *socializing*.

When I wasn't being hounded by someone who wanted to pet me, I climbed the cat tree onto the catio and made myself at home. The window was open and it was the only way I could experience the outdoors again. Volunteers built box platforms off most of the property windows and enclosed them with welded wire, which is just another name for flimsy bars. The parking lot lay right outside the catio, separated from the road by a chain link fence that was always open during visiting hours. I would scratch my head on the welded wire and poke my claws through the holes towards freedom — towards home.

The more time I spent on the catio, the more I wondered if Mother ever made it back. Or my sisters and brothers. Were any of them looking and longing for me as fiercely as I longed for them? I yowled. Another cat gave me a sideways glance and I hissed. He scampered out of the catio as if zapped with static and almost fell off the cat tree on the other side. I pressed my weight into the wire bars and relished feeling the metal combing through my fur.

I combed the wire in return, first with the pads of my paws, then with my claws. *Ting-ting-ting-ting.* The sound lingered on the air like a half formed thought. If only I could shred bars like I shredded bark. Then again, we felines have the dastardly ability to fit our bodies through anything we can get our heads through. I had been thinking about this all wrong. I didn't need to cut through the bars, I needed to cut through *a bar*. Give me three inches and I was homeward bound. I bent down, sniffed, and gave the crisscrossing metal a cursory headbutt. I pushed again with more vigor. Then I shoved. At the base of the catio where the metal welded to the wood was a spot that gave a fur more than the rest. If I subjected it to half as much "socializing" as I was getting, it would open up to me in no time.

Every uninterrupted moment went into sawing that skinny strip of metal. I anticipated a week's worth of work, but the bar caved to my demands in a manner

Maxine: Feline Road to Recovery

of days. I wriggled between the wire and the base and landed in a small planter area under the catio. The sensation of soil and pebbles beneath my paws gave me whispery tingles down my back. I glanced at the catio; the wire fell back against the base so you couldn't tell it was ever moved unless you pushed on it. By the time they noticed I was missing, I would be home.

There was just one problem: blacktop. I'd only encountered blacktop up close and personal once or twice before, and at the time it was frozen from the cold winter weather. Now it was June. The second I stepped onto the parking lot I feared my toe pads were going to liquefy. I yanked my paw back and licked it indignantly. I'd have to wait for that infernal human creation to cool down before I could make my journey. At least there were plenty of places around the property to hide while I passed the time. Little did I know the blacktop was only the first of many problems getting home.

I found an old, beat-up kiddie stage around the back of the property and crawled deep into the shadows. As nice as a sunbath was, the risk wasn't worth the reward. Hours passed and I emerged to a twinkling sky. A canine whined in the dark and cars grunted around the casino the next street over. The blacktop was warm to the touch, but even with my superb night vision it was too dark to start my trip. On top of that, it was *cold*. The temperature had dropped at least thirty degrees since my escape and a nasty draft found its way under the stage. Mother always said Nevada weather changed at the flick of a tail. My siblings and I never understood what she meant. Not because we were Manxes, but because it was so cold for the first three-and-a-half months of our lives.

    I scoured the gated grounds in search of something snug and inconspicuous. The tree was scalable, but I knew from experience cold branches weren't particularly comfortable. No, that wouldn't do, nor would the empty clay planters near the front door. I passed Linda's old El Camino and was surprised by the sensation of warm breath on my face. The Camino felt like one of the many space heaters scattered throughout Catmandu, but several times as large. I arched my head and back along the corner of the bumper. Perfect. Underneath the vehicle was even warmer still.

    I finally understood why neighborhood cats liked to sprawl out on the hoods of newly parked cars at night. I couldn't risk being seen on a hood, but the thought gave me an idea: what if I hid *under* the hood? Mother used to have a hissing fit over the things I wedged myself into when I was young. I clawed up the throat of the Camino and discovered a feline-sized cubbyhole beneath the fan belt. I tucked myself into a meatloaf and gave in to sleep.

    Clink, clink.

    Lizards don't jingle. Why was that lizard jingling? The lizard in question took cover under a bundle of sagebrush. I looked at my sisters but they didn't seem to notice that our prey was making metallic noises, and if they did, the anomaly didn't concern them. I opened my mouth to voice my concerns and the ground started rumbling. An earthquake? No, worse than an earthquake. My eyes cracked open to slats of flaxen light

Maxine: Feline Road to Recovery

peering through the Camino's hood and the vibrations of someone moving around inside the vehicle. I had been dreaming. The jingling wasn't a lizard at all. It was a set of car keys!

The sound of a car starting from the inside sounds akin to a raging campfire and you're the log trapped in the middle. I leapt from the cubbyhole but I was not swift enough and the fan belt caught my left hind leg. The belt dragged me backwards and my leg made the sound of exploding air pockets on old wood. My stomach seized. Adrenaline momentarily anesthetized my body and I lurched forward with the same fuel that launched me across a cage when one of the guards, Laurie, tried to pet me my first week at Catmandu. There's a human saying that cats always land on our feet and in my experience that was true, so I was unprepared for the crunch of my chin's formal introduction to blacktop. I felt like a juicy sneeze sprayed on the ground and probably looked like one too. Trying to stand landed me sideways and I saw the jagged cut of bone unsheathed from my skinned hindquarters. I swallowed several yowls in fear of discovery. The pain was, well, I can't say because I have never experienced an equivalent. I will admit I'm a devout atheist, but in that moment even I issued a prayer to the Goddess of Cats, Bastet, on the off chance She might relieve some part of my anguish. Needless to say, my mewls went unanswered.

The engine died and the driver's door squealed. Never mind my leg, I did not go through the effort of escaping to go right back to confinement. I forced myself into triangular balance on my three un-shattered legs and galloped. Behind me the nails of my dead leg dragged against the blacktop making a sound like grinding teeth. I made it around the side of the building and collapsed onto the right side of my body. I could barely make out Linda opening the hood of the Camino.

"What on earth..." A storm of my missing calico fur hailed her and she swatted it away with an agility any feline would be proud of. "Oh my God. Max! *Maxine?*" She leaned so far over the engine I thought she was going to fall inside. Her chest eased upon realizing I wasn't there, but the relief didn't last. She searched around the car for a blood trail, but somehow I'd outrun my wound. "Where *are* you?"

It's a good thing Linda left out bowls of "feral food." Nothing fancy like Friskies, just the edible pebbles. At night, I dragged myself out from under my hiding spot in the stage to steal what I could from the feral bowls and sip from puddles, if I could find any. I heard Linda host search party after search party for me. Sometimes volunteers even walked right over the stage never knowing I was underneath, counting their footsteps. Dirt and cobwebs embedded themselves in my wound and compounded my agony. Sometimes I woke to the tickle of ants peppering my festering skin.

"It's been two weeks," Linda said from somewhere in the backyard. "With all the fur that came out of the engine, I'm afraid we're looking for a body at this point. If you smell anything, let me know."

Maxine: Feline Road to Recovery

Oh, I smelt all right, so I followed up on her request the next day. I can't even tell you why, but I crawled out from the stage and meowed at the top of my lungs until my wails lured Linda outside. She tilted her head and her face scrunched up at first, then her eyes bulged in a way that reminded me of the expression my sister made before she pounced on someone. I suddenly regretted my decision and burrowed back under the stage. She couldn't get to me, but now she knew where I was, and no doubt the rest of the guards would too by morning.

Speaking of morning, I inched out before sunrise to discover a familiar sight: a metal box with a plate of Friskies at the back. My stomach screamed. Fool me once, shame on me. Fooling me twice wasn't happening. This time I entered of my own volition. It was a win for both of us, you see: I gave them the pleasure of thinking they'd tricked me and kept my pride intact by not allowing them to apprehend me using their smelly human hands. Mind you, the hands off approach only lasted the drive to the next town where they rushed me to the single veterinarian open on the weekend. I don't remember anything after the encroaching cloud of latex fingers.

The worst thing about waking up without your leg — aside from the excruciating amputation pain — is the inability to scratch one's ear. Maybe the point is null because even if I could have scratched myself I was restrained with something called a "cone of shame." The indignity of getting caught by the fan belt had nothing on this fresh humiliation. Even Mother never scratched my own itches for me! Linda, on the other hand...had a very good hand indeed. But her feathery scrubs didn't get a chance to develop into anything more substantial. Four days after the amputation, the incision in my abdomen was oozing puss and decay and I had to go back for a second surgery, lucky me.

Well, I say "surgery," but I believe the technical term is "botch job." First of all, my stitches were put in too tight — and given the chance I would've put my claws in too tight to the man responsible, but the opportunity never arose. Second of all, necrosis. You would *think* that if the tissue around a wound is turning black you *might* want to remove said tissue. But no, this "doctor" merely cleaned out the puss and zipped me back up. Never mind that he did not provide a way for my wound to drain the first *or* second time I had the displeasure of going under his knife. Just scoop out the snotty green infection and all is golden, right? To be fair, everything started looking golden — or was it jaundiced? Who can tell the difference when you're running a fever that could make a sun god sweat? Right about that time I started feeling too listless to eat.

Linda drove me to Washoe Valley Veterinary Services next. "I don't think she can take another intensive surgery so soon," she told the staff. I guess she was starting to understand me better than I expected because I most certainly was not up to being cut open for the third time. Dr. Fisher concurred and brought in one of her new hires, Dr. Peck, to collaborate on a treatment plan.

Maxine: Feline Road to Recovery

"I saw something like this in veterinary school," Dr. Peck said. "If we can pack the wound with saline soaked gauze, we might be able to draw out the infection."

They removed the decaying skin, cleaned me up, and strapped their saline solution to my abdomen like a bow on a Christmas package. Linda and her volunteers worked tirelessly to change my bandages several times a day. Clever young Dr. Peck was right: it drained the infection in ten days. I was still shackled with the cone of shame, however. The volunteers took turns scratching my ears and neck for me. Some even dared to stroke my back and I let them get away with it.

"You like scritches?" Linda asked.

I looked at her like she'd grown a tail. *If I didn't like them*, I thought, *I'd swat you*. Her hand fell away and I had an epiphany. I lifted my paw and smacked her right on the hand like you might do to a naughty human child. She raised an eyebrow and I met it with an impassive stare.

"More scritches?"

Obviously. I trained the volunteers with equal speed and moved into the Catmandu lobby for maximum scrubs. This meant I was one of the first felines humans saw when they walked through the front door. Given the visual nature of humans, I wasn't thrilled to be the object of their gaze. Humans stare. A lot. Even a bit of grass, or "salad" as Linda calls it, between another human's teeth is a cause for staring.

"What happened to that one?"

"That's Max. She escaped and had an accident under the hood of my car."

Rescued Volume 2

"Poor baby."

"Oh, you'd be surprised! Maxine gets around on those three legs. She's a trooper."

I didn't like my missing leg to be the salad between my teeth and Mark Wahlworth was my solution. He donated a cat tree one afternoon and it sat in the lobby while Linda decided where to move it. I made the decision for her. She looked rather pleased when I shot up the tree and planted myself on the throne at the top.

"I guess it's staying in the lobby," she said.

Right there, Human, that's a good spot, right behind my ear. How apt, because you have been an exquisite listener. I'm impressed by your patience and to answer your question, yes, you may come back and visit me. As you've heard, I have had quite a few detours and wrong turns to get where I am now, though I suppose I could be open to a new direction. But no speeding or I might just run right back home…to Catmandu. In the meantime, continue with that scrubbing and we'll see where the road takes us.

ALLIE: MY FAIR KITTEN

Human grief has a particular odor. It's harsh, acrid and unforgettable. I first smelled it on a summer day in a trailer park on the outskirts of town. It was the day the woman was abandoned.

My siblings were playing among the weeds that bordered the property. I was curled under the shade of a nearby bush, batting at my new treasure. It had fallen from around the woman's neck days earlier. It lay there, glittering, colors dancing enticingly when the sunlight struck it. My paws fairly itched to have it.

Its acquisition had been a monumental task for someone of my small stature. Its faceted surface, though cracked, had proven impossible to grip with tooth or claw. But I was determined. The colony crone, a weathered tabby with a milky eye and tattered ear, had cackled in amusement as I sent it flipping and tumbling under the direction of paw and nose. I thought of the woman that had dropped it, whose voice we now heard raised in entreaty. She smelled...she smelled the way the new cat in our colony had smelled when he realized his humans were not coming back for him.

We froze as a man's angry voice rang out, shattering the afternoon calm. The woman softly wept as footsteps crunched hard against the gravel. We made ourselves small and slunk further into the brush as he headed for the not-alive monster he called "truck," sitting under the trailer park's lone tree.

We knew to run when the monster awoke from its slumber. It had been a lesson learned at the expense of my litter-brother's life during a harsh Missouri winter. I felt deeply offended that something with such delicious warmth could turn on us so easily. Yes, when the not-alive thing awoke, we knew to run.

My littermates ran for the woods. I ran for the trailer.

None of the colony cats understood my fondness for that trailer. Except for the occasional field mouse found scurrying beneath its belly, there wasn't much of interest there. The odds of finding a scrap of food were nonexistent compared to the bounty often found in the big container the humans called "dumpster" at the end of the road.

The colony crone, she knew. She sat in the shadows one day as I wriggled my small frame through the latticework skirting the trailer and trotted over to my special spot. She watched as I lay there, staring up at the thing I wanted most in the world.

Allie: My Fair Kitten

I'd found it quite by accident, while chasing a chipmunk on its way to the woods. I stopped short when the image of a cat with long, luxurious fur grabbed my attention. She — it was surely a she! — peered out at me from a torn page covering a hole in the trailer's floor. She sat on a divan, glittery things draped elegantly around her neck. Next to her sat a graceful silver bowl containing more food than I had seen in one place my entire life.

This — *this!* — was my destiny. I determined at that moment that I was going to be that cat. I found myself slipping away from my siblings to steal another glimpse of what now had become my dream, my goal.

"I see you, girlie," came the raspy voice from the shadows. It was the crone. Where had she come from? I hadn't heard a whisper of movement, yet here she was. Impressive, given her age. Being all of eight months old myself, I was certain no cat could sneak up on me, yet she had.

The crone had to be at least seven or eight, which meant she was a good four years older than any other cat in the colony. She frequently turned her wisdom to her advantage, trading bits of sage advice for the occasional mouse parts or nibble of stale hamburger scavenged from the trash.

"I see you, girlie. And I see what you come under here to stare at. You think that cat is real?" She hacked, drew in a wheezing breath and pointed a chipped yellowed claw at me. "Fancies like that don't exist except in pretend images, and mooning after such things will just bring you disappointment."

"That's not true!" I nosed my head in the direction of the images. "The human above us has sparkly things. Why can't I?"

The crone cackled a laugh. "That human is no different than any one of us, girlie. She catted around with a tom and he left her, just as will happen when you come of age. And now she has a kitten of her own on the way. It'll be the same for you, mark my words!"

"Never! I'll never be like my dam," I declared passionately, "yowling after old One Ear, then growing bigger and slower every day!" I shuddered. "I'm *never* having kittens. *Ever.*"

The crone just shook her head and crawled slowly out from under the trailer.

I turned back, gazing once again at the cat on the divan. The edges of the paper fluttered a bit, caught by a stray breeze.

"I'm going to leave here," I told the image. "I am." I whispered the vow quietly to myself. "I'm going to *have* things that sparkle. And food in a beautiful bowl, just like you." The cat stared back, unblinking.

I had never been more miserable. Ever. I hadn't even made it to my first birthday when I was consumed by this awful, restless, achy feeling. Worse, the crone shot me knowing looks as I paced restlessly.

"Well, I'm sorry," I glared at her, "it's damned uncomfortable!" I yowled my frustration as I stalked past her, then slammed to the ground, rubbing my face against the cool dirt to ease my distress.

Allie: My Fair Kitten

The crone squinted at the sun, now low in the horizon. "Won't be too many more sleeps before you'll be growing a litter in your belly." She shot an "I-told-you-so" look my way.

"I didn't *ask* for this," I growled between clenched fangs. "And I don't want any babies of my own. I'm too young!"

🐾 🐾 🐾

A gentle hand ran down my back as one of the little creatures inside me gave a healthy kick. Ow! That *hurt*. I looked up as the woman with glittery things sat beside me on the front steps of the trailer. "They're active tonight," she murmured, the other hand held against her own gravid belly.

Once she realized I shared the same fate she did, the woman had gone out of her way to make me comfortable. Piles of kibble appeared before her door twice a day. I even managed to grab a few bites, if I could beat the colony cats to it. Then each day, when the sun began to wane, she would carefully maneuver down the trailer steps to sit at the bottom. Her hands often fiddled restlessly at her throat, the shiny gems of her necklace catching in the setting sun.

I'd always been a sucker for shiny things.

I would sidle up to her ungainly bulk and rest my own next to her. And she would stroke my back slowly. Two females, trapped in the same sad situation.

"You're lucky, you know?" she said softly to me. "You only have to suffer for 9 weeks. I have to endure this for 9 months." A small shudder rippled through me that had nothing to do with the things moving around in my belly. That was almost exactly as long as I'd been on this earth. I was abruptly glad I hadn't been born human.

"What am I going to do with you?" she asked. I looked up but she was staring off in the distance, lost in thought. "I can't afford to take care of you and the kittens." She looked down at me. "And I can't let the landlord see them once they're born. We've been lucky with the other cats so far, but people have begun to complain. He might take them to the river and — " A tiny dribble of water ran down her cheek in that strange way humans have, and I caught the faintest whiff of grief scent. She shut her eyes tightly and scrubbed angrily at her face. "Stupid hormones!"

A sigh, and then the hand renewed its slow stroke down my back.

Our routine continued unchanged until the day she suddenly jumped up, squealing. "Fleas!" She began flapping her dress, hopping madly from one foot to the other, and then lumbered up the steps as rapidly as she could. The next evening as I leaned against her, she grabbed me firmly and began running this…sharp thing…down my back. "Sorry, sorry," she told me as I struggled to break free. "I was afraid to put flea medicine on you, being pregnant and all. Besides," she added under her breath, "who knew it was so *expensive*…."

I stayed away from her for three sleeps after that. My beautiful, lush fur coat — shaved off! And the nights were growing cooler. By way of apology, she brought a cardboard box lined with towels and set

Allie: My Fair Kitten

it under the trailer in the shadow of the steps, then coaxed me over to it with an extra handful of kibble. Just in time, too.

The blast of a horn roused me from my exhausted stupor as one of those not-alive monsters came to a halt in a spray of gravel. I watched from my cardboard box as two small humans emerged, voices jeering loudly as they raced toward the trailer. A voice rose in harsh reprimand as the monster disgorged its third occupant. The boys ignored her as she approached, too engaged in wrestling each other to the ground. One of them landed hard against the side of the trailer just a few feet from my box. The trailer door above me opened.

"I didn't know you were coming," I heard the glittery woman say. The timbre of her voice and the faintest whiff of anger told me she was not pleased to see them.

The mid-September afternoon settled back into its rhythms. The cicadas once again began to drone, and the crickets resumed their chirping. I sighed and wearily climbed out of the box. It seemed I was always hungry these days. My weight had dropped in the weeks following the kittens' birth, and the handfuls of kibble the woman gave me weren't enough to sustain us. I needed to hunt.

The kittens began crying as I returned. I was climbing into the box when the trailer door slammed open and the small humans came racing down. I jerked my head up, instinctively backing away at the sudden loud noise — and accidentally stepped on one of the babies, who emitted a piercing squeak.

"Did you hear that?"

"Kittens!"

The boys ran toward my nest, one of them grabbing a stick as he came. They crowded close and I hissed at them in warning just as the glittery woman warned, "Stay back, don't hurt them!"

The boys ignored her and the one with the stick poked it at me. I growled and swiped at it, catching the soft flesh of his hand as he withdrew with a howl. He dropped the stick as the glittery woman pulled him away. He kicked out toward the box but she held him back with one hand, the other pressed protectively against her own rounded belly.

"She's just a mama cat protecting her babies," I heard her say "It'll be fine if you just leave her be."

"You have a stray cat sleeping under your *trailer*? She *bit* my boy! She could have *rabies!*" The strange woman shrieked so loudly, I flattened my ears in discomfort.

Allie: My Fair Kitten

I'm not certain who was more shaken by the experience, me or the glittery woman. Once they left she turned to examine the kittens in the box.

"Pretty girl," she murmured, "what am I to do with you?"

🐾 🐾 🐾

The blue of the day gave way to dusk's indigo, and I settled in with the kittens for a quiet night. Suddenly the box closed above me and everything turned black. I heard the ripping noises of hands taping the box shut and I yowled in protest, scratching futilely at the lid.

"It'll be okay," the glittery woman's voice whispered softly. "Shh-h-h." The box moved as she carried me toward one of the not-alive monsters that sat rumbling in the parking lot, its sound growing louder as we approached. "We're going for a short ride in Alfred's car, that's all." The box jostled slightly as she opened the door and settled inside.

I smelled the scent of the kindly older man from the trailer at the end of the row. The few times we saw him, he always had a bit of something to toss our way — food, or a wad of paper to bat about.

"It's for the best," his gruff voice said reassuringly as the glittery woman sniffled.

I could feel the monster begin to move, but the gentle swaying did nothing to ease my fears. A few moments later, it rolled to a stop and the woman lifted our box. I began wailing in earnest as I sensed unfamiliar surroundings, and the glittery woman crooned softly as she walked. She rested the box against a hard surface, and whispered a watery, "Goodbye." I felt the scrape of her fingers as she softly brushed the box's lid, then heard her footsteps as she turned and walked back to the car. A door slammed and the monster rolled away.

The box had little insulation, just threadbare towels lining the bottom — and of course, the warmth of four squalling babies. The breeze gusted in through the slits of the box, bringing with it the smells of coyote and fox. They were old scents but still worrisome.

The little I could see told me the woman had set my box against a hard, human-made surface. I hoped the human smell that permeated the area would be deterrent enough for any predator. Not that it mattered. Even though I shoved my nose hard against the lid, it remained firmly taped shut. And with the babies pressed so close around me, I couldn't very easily claw my way out.

Another gust buffeted the box lightly and drew a shiver down my back where the woman had shaved my coat. Without the warmth of four tiny bodies huddled close against mine, it would have been much chillier. I itched terribly from the fur growing back in — and the fleas that were still there. Why had she left me? I had stayed mostly out of the way these past weeks, except for that one excruciating night the kittens had been born.

I settled in as best I could as the kittens burrowed close. The little bowl of kibble placed in the box earlier that evening was long empty. I tried to ignore the scrabbling of field mice in the bushes nearby, but the gnawing in my stomach made this unattainable food

Allie: My Fair Kitten

source difficult to ignore. It was going to be a long, watchful night. Yet despite my best efforts, I felt sleep pulling at me.

An approaching sound brought me fully alert. Sleeping kittens scattered as I rose to a crouch and peered through one of the slits. I trembled slightly as I watched a truck pull up, similar to the one that had belonged to the angry man so many months ago.

A car pulled up next to it, and two humans stepped out, voices carrying faintly on the breeze. One inhaled deeply. "Smells like fall, Sharon," one of the women said. "Cricket would agree with you," the other one agreed. "She was pretty frisky this morning when I got u—" She broke off as she saw the box that held us captive.

"Ann? See that?"

They slowed as the one called Ann nodded slowly. She sighed. "After last week, I don't think I can bear it if I open that box and the poor thing...."

Sharon looked over at the man exiting the truck.

"Doctor Pickett!" She raised her voice and pointed toward my box.

The man looked up at Sharon's hail, then slammed the truck's door and jogged toward me and the kittens.

This was not good. The two women I could tolerate. Maybe. But someone who appeared in a monster machine like the one that killed my littermate? And he was approaching almost aggressively. I could smell the anger, too. No, this was not good.

"Hang on," he called out. "I'll open it." He tore at the material that held the box closed, short angry movements punctuated by harsh words at each swipe.

He stopped abruptly, rocking back on his heels as he lifted the flap and gazed down at me. Instantly, his eyes softened.

"It's okay." He spoke gently now, addressing the others. "A mom and four kittens." He squinted into the shadowed recesses of the box, then carefully lowered a hand and scooped a kitten up. "A bit snotty. URI, but alive."

I refused to take my eyes off the man but could hear the women as they simultaneously released held breath. Both slowly approached and crouched near the box, one of them crooning softly as she held my gaze, blinking slowly. I felt myself relaxing the slightest bit.

The box was lifted as they moved us into the human structure. One of the women reached out in a flicking motion and light, bright and harsh, caused me to duck my head. The smell of many animals assaulted my senses. I could feel my hackles begin to rise. Was I being thrust into some other colony's territory? Would I have to fight my way into being accepted?

The rhythm of the human carrying me slowed. With a slight creak, a door opened and we were in another place with entirely different smells. There were animals whose scents indicated illness as well as sharp, astringent scents that were unfamiliar. The box came to rest and the lid once again opened.

"Let's see what we have here," the man's voice had grown exceedingly soft and when he reached a hand toward one of the kittens, he did it so slowly I sensed no threat. Cupping her tiny body in his hands, he raised her up, then pressed a shiny silver thing up against her chest and listened for a moment. Turning, he handed her to

Allie: My Fair Kitten

a woman standing next to him. The process repeated itself three more times and then he turned to me.

"Hello, little mama. Let's see how you're faring today, shall we?"

🐾 🐾 🐾

Much of what happened next was a blur: cold exam tables, intense sleepiness, a bit of soreness, and then lovely warmth. Hours of quiet aloneness, caged in a metal box with a small piece of sand in one corner and a bowl of water in another. And food! Food that kept coming. Every. Single. Day. And the fleas? Gone.

One of the humans who fed me told me they had taken my kittens to a place called "foster." Call me callous, but I didn't miss them in the least. I'd never wanted kittens, nor to be trapped in the same circumstances as my dam, an endless cycle of motherhood season after season. Yet I had. And somehow, through the seeming betrayal of my glittery woman, it had all changed.

Weeks passed and they moved me to the part of the structure that smelled of a cat colony — and yet not. I could smell dozens of cats, but it wasn't the scent of a cohesive unit. They had an aura of displacement, like me.

That first night in the new place, I heard a sibilant noise from the metal box next to mine.

"Sssst! New female, hello, can you hear me?" It was the voice of a tom.

"Who are you, and where is this place?" I whispered back.

"You're at a place called Shelter, in the land of Wayside. And you, little one, are a Waif."

Perhaps his dam had dropped this tom on his head when he was a kitten. I'd heard that could addle a cat.

"Tomorrow morning, humans will arrive," he continued. "They will open your kennel — the metal box you're sitting in. They will rub you and coo at you and then go on to the next kennel and repeat the ritual. The lucky ones here are the cats who make a connection with a human."

"What do you mean, connection?"

"Have you never had a human of your own, little one?" he asked gently. "Did you not come from a place you called home?"

"Well, yes, I mean — I had the colony, that was home. Me and my dam and the crone, and my litter mates...."

"Ahh-h-h," he said in a long exhale. "You were an outdoor cat, then. A community cat. Did they tip your ear?"

I frowned in puzzlement. "Did they what?"

"Did they cut the tip off one of your ears?" he asked. "They do that to mark what they call ferals." I quickly swiped both ears with my paw but they didn't feel any different. "No-o-o," I replied slowly. "They feel the same."

"Good," he said. "They must feel you'll have no problem connecting with a human."

The tom's words jumbled in my head, confused bits of information that made little sense to me. He must have sensed this, because he began purring in reassurance. "You sound like a sharp girl. You'll catch on quickly. Just follow my lead and you'll do fine."

The tom was right. As the days passed, humans trooped through, dangling bits of fur or holding treats invitingly, and I began to notice a pattern.

Allie: My Fair Kitten

I watched as cats in nearby metal boxes — kennels, I corrected myself — were approached, stroked and spoken to gently by humans. I saw them respond with head-butts and purrs. I saw them gathered in human arms and held close, while words of love and phrases like "forever home" and "adoption" were spoken.

I heard stories from fellow residents — cats who shared tales of a lifetime of love and companionship, who experienced a bond with a human that had been broken only by death. I smelled their grief, witnessed the compassion of a human touch, and I saw hope begin to grow that maybe, just maybe, another human companion might be found. Not to replace the one the cat had lost, but to fill the loneliness.

Loneliness. I'd been a rather independent sort in my one year of life. There really hadn't been time to be lonely. I was too busy surviving. But here, in this kennel, I began to feel that this "forever home" might be something I'd like, too. Perhaps...perhaps I might even find a human who would serve me meals in stemmed silver dishes, one who liked glittery things like I did. I decided it was time to take my destiny into my own paws. I would actively begin seeking my perfect human.

When the lights went on the following morning, my first order of the day was to inform the shelter staff it was my turn to free roam about the facility. I began to pace inside my confined area, calling out for attention. It worked. A cart pushed into view from around the corner and the human behind it greeted me.

"A little restless this morning, are we?" she asked. "Want out to roam a bit?" I pawed enthusiastically at the kennel door, cooing a bit in praise of this human's insightfulness. The door swung open and I jumped down. Spying a bright red ball under a nearby bench, I wandered over to begin batting it about and waiting for humans to start arriving.

The day passed without any decent prospects. I dutifully examined each human who entered, but none were right for me. Not the next day, nor the day after. And so it went, this pattern of searching, until it became routine. Some of the staff began to voice sympathy for my plight. "Poor little thing," I heard them say. "It's because she's been shaved that she keeps getting passed by. Don't they know her fur will grow back?"

One day, not long after the outside had turned gray and the trees had dropped their leaves, the humans known as "volunteers" began decorating the room. There were colorful dangly things that swooped high up out of paw's reach, bright garlands of red and green with twinkly lights like fireflies dancing in their depths. Music came from little black boxes overhead and the volunteers were exchanging gaily-wrapped bags and boxes of things. And the visiting humans? Some of them wore the oddest things. There were jingly bells attached to woven-fur tops instead of properly attached to the toys we liked to bat around. Some had long red things perched atop their heads with white balls at their pointy ends. Balls, I might add, that were better suited for rolling loose on the floor to be chased. Humans could be so very strange.

Allie: My Fair Kitten

Just a hair after the sun in the sunroom reached its zenith, *he* came in. Tall and dark, accompanied by a younger one who looked much like him, and a woman who I immediately dismissed as unimportant.

I grabbed the nearest bell toy and casually made my way toward them, batting the ball between my paws as if it were the most important thing in the world. I pounced just as I reached their location, sending the ball flying with a sharp jingle. The younger one pointed to me and asked, "What about that one?"

The tall man kneeled and held out his hand to me, inviting me to sniff. A proper gentleman! It appeared I had chosen well.

The woman with them struck up a conversation with the volunteers, asking about my shorn fur. They assured her this was something a human had done to me, and not a disease. My pelt would soon return to its luxurious state.

As the women talked, I got to know my human. He knew just how to rub and scratch in all the right places. And the younger one said the nicest things about me — how friendly and intelligent I was, and how pretty my markings were. And then the woman pulled him away. She pulled *my* human from me — to show him other "candidates."

"Looks like you were just rejected Miss Gray."

The old tom who had kenneled next to me had been adopted a week earlier, and in his place sat a rotund, long-haired hussy.

"I'm sure they'd prefer to have a cat with *fur* after all," she smirked. She turned away, grooming her left shoulder in a clear snub that would have ended with her fat behind being bitten had she not been safely sealed inside her kennel.

Fuming, I turned, and bumped squarely into old buff-and-white Mister Anderson. I hissed and swatted at him in frustration. I felt a bit bad about that. Anderson was a sweet soul who had happened upon me at just the wrong moment. The hussy in the old tom's cage with her catty remarks wasn't his fault. I took a deep breath and trotted off toward my human.

As I rounded the corner, the young one spied me, pointed and said, "That's the one you want, right there." *Listen to the boy*, I silently urged.

My human turned and lifted me into his arms. I purred and rubbed against him, and then squirmed to be set down. It was time to impress him with my skills! I batted furiously at the wand toy the young human held, forcing it into submission and going for the kill. I flipped coyly onto my back and batted my eyes up at him. He smiled down at me and I knew this was it. I was going home.

When I was carried through the door to my new home, I caught the whiff of an old cat. The room where I spent my first few weeks reeked of him, and I could hear him snuffling and pawing at the other side of the door at odd hours.

"Who *are* you?" I asked in annoyance after it became clear he was not going away.

Allie: My Fair Kitten

"My name is Ryker, and this is *my* home," the muffled voice announced to the carpet at my paws. "You're not welcome here."

"Well, the human chose me," I hissed back. "So I am *too* welcome!"

"I was here first," he growled. "I've been with my Person since I was a kitten and you can't have her!"

"Her?" I replied angrily. "I don't want *her*. The other one is mine. I chose him, he chose me!"

Silence came from the other side of the door as Ryker paused. "AlphaPerson?" he finally exclaimed. "He did?"

The man that Ryker called AlphaPerson spent many hours in the room with me, feeding me, playing, petting. "What are you going to call her?" the woman asked as she accompanied him into the room one afternoon. He stood, waving a wand toy for me, thinking.

"It needs to be a majestic name," he said finally. "Look at those ears, they stand so straight and tall. As if she were some Egyptian princess." They both looked musingly at me, lost in thought. After a moment, my human suggested tentatively, "Alexandria?"

The woman tilted her head, examining me as I looked back at her. "As in Alexandria, Egypt? The great intellectual city of the ancient world?"

He nodded.

"And we could call her Allie for short. Allie, Allie-cat."

He frowned at that. I turned and scowled at her, too. I was no alley cat. Not any more.

"She's my Allie-girl," he said firmly. That, I could live with.

Rescued Volume 2

    I eventually came face-to-face with Ryker, the old cat who laid claim to the woman. He was stuffy, a bit curmudgeonly, and very set in his ways. He was also a rather fastidious purebred, a chocolate point Tonkinese who never, ever let me forget my "common roots." Oh, and did I mention he was loud? Perhaps he was hard of hearing, having reached the ripe old age of thirteen, because he yowled at me incessantly.
    It was such fun to pounce on him. To tear through the house and disturb his sleep. To block his passage through the halls. I became the mistress of sneak attacks, until one day the woman came home to find him cowering under a desk. When he flinched away from her hand, she examined him more closely, and found a tattoo of puncture marks on his head.
    Let me make myself perfectly clear. He ran into my extended claws. I hadn't intended to connect with his head when I swiped. Besides, any decently agile cat would have zigged when he zagged. I tried to apologize, but he just cringed when I approached and slunk away. Not too long after that, I received my very first pedicure.
    Hot pink nail caps — SoftClaws, they were called — looked magnificent with my grey and white tuxedo coat. My human took one look at me and declared I needed a collar to match. We went shopping online for one together, and I made my preference for shiny things quite clear. Not too long after, I sported this lovely thing of pink velvet with brilliantly gleaming white crystals.
    I sat in the room where I had first been confined, staring at my reflection in the mirror. Turning my head

Allie: My Fair Kitten

this way and that, I watched as the afternoon light caught the shiny things, causing them to dance in the sun. Was this truly me? Though my fur had yet to fully grow back, I no longer looked gaunt and exhausted. That reality seemed at once to be both yesterday and a lifetime ago.

As the weeks went on, we settled into a routine, me and my human. The woman had taken to calling me the "other woman." She laughingly informed my human he had his own little Princess who, she was sure, called him "Father." I didn't care what words they used, as long as they both understood the bond he and I shared. Our routine consisted of mornings at the computer, me stretched out along the length of his legs or snuggled up next to his heart.

I still chased the old mancat around the house, on principle. In my defense, it was the only exercise he ever engaged in, as the rest of his time was spent napping on the bed.

My collar wardrobe increased, too. I became the proud owner of a lovely strand of pink pearls, a ridiculous pink tulle monstrosity that made my neck look fat, and a lovely faux ruby ensemble. And then, after a weekend afternoon when the humans had been off "shopping," *it* arrived.

Although my human urged the woman to show it to me, she began preparing our food instead. At the time I thought she might be stalling, but as a cat who knows what it's like to be hungry I could appreciate her priorities. It was within a few hours of dinnertime, after all.

But then she set the food before me…in a footed silver bowl.

I sat there for a brief moment, stunned. It wasn't *the* bowl from the tattered paper image tucked under that trailer floor a lifetime ago. Its lines were different, its shape and cut unique. No, it wasn't the bowl from my long-ago dreams. It was far better. Because it was *real*. And it was mine.

Human happiness has a particular odor. It smells of sunshine and spring breezes. It is altogether pleasant and it permeated my new home. And if humans had noses with enough sensitivity, they would have been able to smell feline happiness, musky and soft. I was happy. I was home.

A few weeks shy of our one-year anniversary, I was napping in a sun puddle by the back door. My human was out raking leaves in the late November afternoon. The woman was folding clothes by the dryer. And the old cat, Ryker, was napping by the fireplace. Suddenly, he yowled.

This, in itself, was not an unusual occurrence. He often aired his grievances, and they came in many different forms, from an empty bowl to his Person's lap not being available. This time, though, it was a yowl of pain — and it didn't let up. The woman called out to my man and they rushed to Ryker's side. Within moments, they had bundled him into one of her sweaters and rushed out the door.

Allie: My Fair Kitten

Human grief has a particular odor. It's harsh, acrid and unforgettable.

My man and his woman came in smelling of this later that evening. And they came back without Ryker. That's when I knew.

The man is most definitely *mine*. But on that night, that one and only time, I crawled up onto the woman, just as that old mancat did. I carefully placed my paws on her chest, just as I'd seen him do countless times. I rested my head near her heart.

And I purred for her.

WU KITTY: RESCUED FROM THE ROW

They say orange is the new black, right? Well, given the death rate for black dogs and cats in the animal shelter system, this wasn't a good thing for an orange cat like me. When I got dumped at New York City's Animal Care and Control I knew things had gone from bad to worse. On the streets of Manhattan I was "Tigress"…until someone grabbed me and brought me in as a stray and now I was a number. That's what I get for looking for food in all the wrong places. That person probably meant well, but they had no way of knowing what goes on behind these doors.

I heard the ACC workers saying things like "mean," "nasty," and "feral" when they poked at me. They red-tagged me, meaning I was aggressive and very sick, and put me on the list that said regular people couldn't

Wu Kitty: Rescued From The Row

adopt me — a death sentence in this place. I was not exactly the type of cat people would be looking at for their next "Fluffy." I had come to terms with the fact that these would be my last days. But I wasn't going down without a fight. I'm a Tigress! That would make it harder to get out of here, but I didn't care. I was who I was and wouldn't change for anyone.

I looked around at all the poor animal souls. They were defeated. Old, young, just born, injured, sick — it didn't matter, we were all on our way out and it didn't look like the way out would be in a van to a new home; more like into the room of no return. Some of my fellow inmates paced in their cages, anxiously awaiting their fate, almost as if it would be a blessing compared to their current circumstances. Others just cried.

Luckily I had learned a thing or two during my year on the streets. An older tomcat named She-Fe had taken me under his wing. He'd discovered me hanging out in an alley, chasing my tail nonstop. He asked, "What are you doing, young one?"

I explained how I'd read that happiness was located in my tail, so I was trying to catch it so I could be happy forever. She-Fe told me he'd read that same tale written by a wise philosopher, but that I must've missed the end of the story. My dirty ears perked up and I paused to listen.

"Happiness is, in fact, found in your tail," he said. "But you do not need to chase after it, little one. The story explains that chasing after your tail will only wear you out and get you nowhere. But if you go about your daily feline life, happiness will just follow you wherever you go."

"Wow!" I said. "So happiness is with me always. Amazing!"

From that day forward I knew that She-Fe could teach me many lessons. And I had many to learn. We became the perfect student-teacher duo. He tried to instill in me the importance of balance, of staying grounded and in the moment, especially during challenging times. He taught me a mantra that helped when I found myself agitated or fearful. He'd tell me to close my eyes, go to a feeling place and repeat to myself: I am air, I am light, I am water flow. This worked well after hours spent dodging in and out of NYC traffic or running away from the mean neighborhood bullies.

I closed my eyes and pictured She-Fe's kind smile, his wise mournful eyes, his long whiskers, and his left ear with the tip. I knew I needed to try implementing She-Fe's teachings now more than ever before. That I needed to remain calm, grounded, and detached from any outcome. But I had this storm raging inside me and I was so angry with these people for imprisoning me and placing labels on me. I knew who I was! I was the Tigress. I was resilient, stealthy, tough and carefree.

I struggled between mindfulness and madness as the days wore on. I felt worse physically and spiritually, like I was suffocating under the thick feeling of despair hanging in the air. I needed to focus, to remember who I was and believe I had a larger mission to fulfill. I went to the back of my cell, made myself small, and tried to concentrate on feeling rooted even though I could

Wu Kitty: Rescued From The Row

feel no ground beneath my paws — only the cold metal floor reeking with the smell of death. Sleep came, but no peace.

I woke with a start in the back corner of my grim steel cell, feeling worse than ever. I hadn't eaten and my body was weary. I tried with all my might to meditate, the way I'd been taught, when the door suddenly opened and a hand reached out. Instantly, I lost my Zen state, turned and lashed out. I instantly regretted it. *You need to work on your anger*, I chastised myself. *She-Fe would be so disappointed in you.*

Then I saw the hands reach in again, this time with heavy gloves. I realized I might not have many more opportunities to work on that Zen state. It looked as though that long hallway was about to become my destiny. I spit, hissed, and fluffed out in an attempt to look big in my scrawny four-pound body. I lost the battle. The gloved hands scruffed me and shoved me inside some kind of a box. When I bit into it, I recognized the cardboard taste immediately. It tasted like the pizza boxes in the back alleys in Manhattan. Only this box had the faint smell of death, while the pizza boxes smelled like heaven.

I was jostled around and then placed in a waiting area with a bunch of other boxes. I could hear the meowing and howls from those who were scared that they were going to a worse fate. Others were too sick or too frozen in fear to make a noise.

I surveyed my surroundings through the holes in the box. Workers milled about talking. It was hot and I really wanted out of the box, so I started to scratch and bite at the cardboard. This did not make these people happy. One woman shook the box.

"Stop it!" she yelled at me, then muttered under her breath, "I can't believe anyone would want to save this nasty, sick, scrawny cat. She's awful!"

Save? They were saving me? I held my breath, barely allowing the thought into my head: This Tigress is about to be out! I relaxed and tried to meditate, to practice what She-Fe had worked to instill in me on the streets, barely daring to believe that I might soon have a new start. I breathed deeply and repeated to myself, "I am air, I am light, I am water flow." Soon I felt more relaxed and eventually I dozed off to a dreamless sleep.

I woke to the sounds of a van door opening and closing and people talking about transports and adoptions. An overwhelming sense of dread took hold of me. What if where I was going was worse than the streets? What if it was worse than the ACC? What if I was being sold to a lab to have horrible experiments done on me? As quickly as these thoughts entered my mind, I shook them off. This bad habit was what She-Fe used to speak of — monkey mind, when your thoughts took over your reasoning, clarity and ability to focus. I was not going to allow monkey mind to play tricks in my head. The chances of something worse than being listed on death row at the ACC were slim.

We remained parked for what seemed like a lifetime and then the driver hopped back in and started the van. I could smell the remnants of cigarette smoke and I wanted so badly to be released from my

Wu Kitty: Rescued From The Row

cardboard prison. Once again I went back to the lessons She-Fe taught, and I sat quietly and focused on my breath.

We stopped many times that day. I heard dogs, cats, and people, and could smell many different aromas, some pleasant, some not. Some of my fellow animal transport companions became carsick. Many had been ill to begin with, and the trip made them feel even worse.

Eventually we stopped. The driver pulled my box out of the van and placed it on the ground. I felt a slight breeze blow through the tiny holes. It smelled like freedom. The April day was warm and the sounds and smells of spring surrounded me — birds chirping, dogs barking in the distance, and the soothing scent of lilac. Spring, when things bloom and grow — a time of rebirth and new beginnings. Was this my stop? Was this where my new journey would begin?

I snapped out of my trance to the sound of a garage door opening and footsteps on the pavement. Then, a voice.

"Hello, I'm so happy you're finally here. Where is she?"

This woman sounded cheerful, full of positive energy and excited for whoever she was waiting for. An unenthusiastic voice answered directly above me.

"Yes, this is her. She was one of the last animals on the transport. Sorry for the delay. I would be very cautious when you go to take this one out of the box. She's not exactly friendly."

I felt the box rise and realized immediately that I was the "she" the kind voice had asked about. I focused on the positive and placed the driver's negative remarks out of my mind. I was the one this woman was waiting for! *Me!* This person was excited to meet *me*. My heart filled with all the possibilities but I remained guarded, as I knew far too well how humans could turn out to be. I was optimistic but not foolish. Balance. Stay balanced, I told myself. We shall see where this leads.

As the humans exchanged paperwork and I was released to this new individual, I sat quietly in my box. My stomach made gurgling noises, my nose ran and I felt awful. My body ached and I was exhausted in every form of the word — physically, emotionally and spiritually. I heard the driver mention medications, and that I was too sick to be spayed when I was at the ACC. The woman who now held me listened and thanked the driver. She slowly closed the garage door. Beams of sunlight flooded in through the garage windows as we made our way toward a door leading inside the house. I held my breath as she opened the door and we crossed the threshold to my new beginning. I prayed it was a good one.

Immediately I knew other felines and canines occupied this home. I could hear dogs barking upstairs, and I could smell cats. I had mixed feelings about other felines, and as for dogs, well, it depended on the dog. I'd met a nice, young dog on the streets once in Manhattan. We both understood what it was like to be falsely labeled. As a pit bull, Momo knew how difficult it was to live with labels and negative stigma. He'd been left tied to a lamppost when I'd found him. I untied him by biting on the ropes until my teeth bled. He was grateful and sweet, not a "bully" at all. He was nothing like all

Wu Kitty: Rescued From The Row

those horrible things you hear people say about pit bulls and similar breeds.

He was in worse shape than me and I head butted him as we shared an old pizza from the alley dumpster. I talked to him about being labeled a feral, an alley cat and a worthless stray. He told me about his horrible start in a "home" full of dogs bred to engage in horrible acts. I cringe thinking about it, and my heart sinks a little wondering what ever became of that sweet fella. I always found it interesting how dogs and cats could get along and understand one another a lot more than people, especially when they were both left to fend for themselves on the streets.

The woman took me into another area of the home and shut the door behind us. She placed the cardboard box on the floor. I could hear the sounds of classical music playing quietly and the aroma of cat food. I licked my lips thinking about it. She slowly and quietly opened the top of the box. I squinted as the light blinded my eyes. I'd been in that dark box for a long time and it was overwhelming, even though the environment itself was quiet, calming and cozy.

The woman smiled at me and sat quietly as I looked up over the rim of the box. I still had the plastic choke collar on my neck, far too tight with a number written across it in ballpoint pen. More labels. I squinted my eyes in anger thinking about the number. I am not a bar code, or some label that foolish humans place on me! I wanted the collar off but I was reluctant to let the human near me. I sat in the box for a long time deciding what my next move should be.

Eventually the woman spoke. "You want that collar off, don't you?"

I watched her with narrowed eyes, wondering where this was going.

"You want to discard that silly number they gave you, and get rid of the negative label," she went on. "They could never truly understand what a beautiful, strong, resilient feline you are. I do, though. You're safe now. You'll be loved, respected and cherished for who you are, not who others wish you to be. It's true," she said, as if she knew I didn't believe her. "If you're wondering how I was able to rescue you from death row even with your label, it was with the help of a NYC rescue group. I offered to foster you back to health and see how things progressed. Sadly, I see countless animals listed on death row every day. Not only in NYC but nationwide. But you spoke to me for a very important reason." She smiled. "We can discuss that more later. For now, make yourself at home and get some rest. When you're ready we can remove that label around your neck once and for all."

I listened to her and observed the laugh lines around her face, but also the bandana on her head. I noticed she had very little hair and only half of her eyebrows and a few eyelashes. She had kind eyes and a quiet patience about her. I instantly felt as if she understood me on a deeper level than other humans. I believed my rescuer may have fallen on some hard times herself. I wondered what her story was. But for now, she was right. I was exhausted and needed sleep.

I jumped out of the box and quickly hid under a tall table. This was a wise choice, as it had a large cat

Wu Kitty: Rescued From The Row

bed under it with clean, soft, welcoming blankets. The human didn't chase me. She stood up, topped off my water bowl and put some kind of drops in the water, and left a treat for me with something inside it.

"I'll let you settle in," she said. "I'll come back and check on you later."

Once she left the room I took a good look around and decided that I was in a much better place. I nibbled at my food, drank some water, located my commode and then settled into my bed. My bed. That was what she called it, *my* bed. I'd never had a bed before. I thought about who this person could be and why she would want to help me. I woke up many times throughout the night, making sure it had not all been a dream, that I was safe and would not be heading to the room of no return.

My body still ached and I wasn't feeling well. I was very skinny, about to go into heat and had a serious upper respiratory infection. I didn't want to burst the human's bubble but I knew the treat had some kind of pill in it. I figured it must be medicine for my cold. I ate it without incident only because I felt so horrible. Normally I would never engage in such foolish trickery. The human came back several times to check in and I pretended to be asleep. The next morning, she arrived with another human. They both talked to me and were kind enough to provide me the space I required. They brought fresh water, more treats and wet and crunchy food. They scooped my commode and put out a few toys. I was now in full-blown heat, feeling lousy and not wanting to do much but cry.

Rescued Volume 2

I allowed the human to take off the ACC collar. She talked to me while she did.

"I've worn many plastic bracelets over the last few years," she said as she cut off the plastic with the offending numbers. "All with numbers. They were too tight and I had to wear them for too long. I was known as #5060985. They gave me countless labels like chronic, autoimmune, incurable, disabled, ostomate, and bald to name a few. I was scooped up and taken to a place I didn't want to go, and believe me I resisted. For me it was a hospital but equally as scary as the ACC. I was also in a life and death situation and almost died. My ride was in an ambulance from a Connecticut hospital to a Boston hospital, while yours was by car from the streets to a cage. I know we both felt the same though. I could see it in your eyes the moment I saw your photo. I could see the fear, the anger, the sadness, but more importantly the desire to heal and be you again. I saw wisdom, hope and resilience. I saw myself in you."

She tossed the collar into the trash. "I remember looking into the mirror at my hairless reflection with missing organs and new appliances. I'd braced myself against the sink of my hospital bathroom, wobbling on my weak legs and staring at the image in front of me. I was finally getting out after two long months. I remember thinking, *This is a fine mess you got yourself into, #5060985.* I thought about the absurdity of being a number. But I knew it was time to regroup, focus and find a way to keep living. You looked like you wanted to do the same, if you could just get out of your cage and shed your number too."

Wu Kitty: Rescued From The Row

I couldn't believe my ears. I knew I felt the connection. I knew she understood but I hadn't realized how deeply. I did hiss and wiggle a little when out of nowhere she hugged me. But I allowed it to happen because it felt good. And it felt even better to finally be understood. It seemed we both wanted to just be — no numbers, no labels, no scary rooms with people poking at you. It seemed like a special bond had been formed between us before we'd even met.

That bond was sorely tested in the days after my arrival. I bit sometimes. Clawed, too. I wrecked a bookcase, tried to eat paperclips, ripped up furniture and — the worst infraction — urinated in the human's new photo printer — a gift. If I were her, taking me back might have made sense. But she never got mad at me. She told me she understood why I would be angry, fearful and confused.

"I won't give up on you," she said.

Then came the bad news — I needed to go to the vet. This vet must have been pretty brave. Even though I only weighed 4 pounds, I was a spitfire and my reputation preceded me.

I was leery when the human put me in the carrier. In spite of her reassurances, I didn't fully trust her yet. After all my bad behavior, I wouldn't have been surprised if I was being sent back to the ACC. I didn't want to go to the vet, but I wanted to be returned to a cell even less.

Once I arrived at the clinic, I showed everyone how fierce I was by hissing and spitting. Eventually I allowed the vet to help me because she didn't yell or call me names. She even seemed like she wanted me to feel better. Once she was done the human placed me back in the carrier gently, even when I clawed her.

"It's time to go home," she said. I was relieved it was over but what really stuck out for me was the word *home*.

I spent the next few weeks trying to be tough and showing the human who was boss. I continued clawing, biting and swatting, often while dancing on my back paws like a boxer. I ate paper towels, destroyed paperwork and knocked bamboo plants to the floor. I wanted to see if she could take it, if she really could handle the good and bad that raged inside me. Would she just give up like the rest and toss me aside?

Instead, one day she came in and sat on the floor with me and made a call. I pretended to be asleep but I listened to every word.

Wu Kitty: Rescued From The Row

"Yes, I decided that her behaviors are a bit challenging and that perhaps the semi-feral label was more accurate than we thought," I heard her say.

My heart sank and I tried to bite back the anger. This human had lied, too. It was inevitable.

"No, I don't want to send her to a sanctuary. I want to officially adopt her. I want her to stay with us and live out her life being who she is and not have to fear being thrown outside or taken to a kill shelter. I will complete the forms today. Thank you for helping me pull her from death row."

I could hardly believe it. The words chased each other around my brain, new and exciting thoughts I hadn't yet allowed myself to consider: adopt me, forever, safe, loved, accepted for who I am. After my poor behavior and all my challenging moments, she still wanted me. The entire family wanted me.

She hung up the phone and looked at me. I opened my eyes and gazed back at her.

"I realize they called you Pumpkin," she said. "I also know that's not a fitting name for a tigress like yourself. Besides, a rescue kitty named Pumpkin already lives here so that name is taken. I'd like to call you Wu. It's a special name for me. As I told you before I've been dealing with serious health issues for many years and it wasn't until I met my friend and healer Dr. Ming Wu that I really started to get better. Not just physically but emotionally and spiritually as well."

I cocked my head at her, interested now. That was a name fit for a cool cat like me. I could be spiritual if I wanted. I'd already been practicing.

"Dr. Wu's a Chinese medicine doctor, a third generation Chinese herbalist, and a master Tai Chi and Qi Gong practitioner. He studies the Tao Te Ching and has taught me so much — how there's good and bad in everything, like the ocean wave rising up, crashing and rising again. You remind me of that. I think Wu Kitty is the perfect name for you."

I preened a little bit inside, trying it on for size. I didn't really know what Chinese medicine was, but it sounded interesting.

"There's one more reason why I felt drawn to you that night I saw you on the 'To Be Destroyed' list," she added. "I recently lost one of my closest friends. His name was TC and he died suddenly from lymphoma. He'd been rescued out of a feral colony in Massachusetts and I adopted him from the Pat Brody Shelter for Cats. You reminded me of him — that spark, the desire to just be yourself and live life on your own terms. Thank you for coming into my life, Wu. If you decide you like this name we'll keep it. You can let me know. You are who you are and I will respect that always."

With that she touched my head gently and walked out of the room.

She had a teacher just like my She-Fe. She has loved and cared for semi-feral cats like me in the past and honored them for who they were. I wish I'd been able to meet TC. I think we would have been good friends. I silently sent up a prayer thanking him for his spirit's guidance in bringing me and this human together.

Wu Kitty. I tried the name on for size. I liked how I felt when I said it, how it sounded as it floated out into

Wu Kitty: Rescued From The Row

the air. I went to sleep that night feeling like I'd been right all along. I did have a greater purpose and I was determined to fulfill that purpose now more than ever.

Eventually, I met my fellow rescue companions. As I'd guessed, there were both canines and felines. By now, I'd been spayed, officially adopted and given a clean bill of health from my vet. I won't lie — the transition took some time. There were a few bumps, like when I peed on the other human's pillow because I didn't like not being the center of attention. The humans still loved me though, and kept telling me things would be fine.

At first, I didn't understand what toys were and what to do with them. I had to learn to enjoy the catnip carrots, fuzzy mice and balls I could chase around the sunroom floor. The humans also had a long piece of fabric on a stick that they waved around. It was almost like the live prey I hunted when I lived on the streets. My favorite thing to stalk, though, was the red dot. I chased it like the bugs in the alley and I was really fast. The humans thought I was fancy with my high jumps and battle cries as I leapt to and fro in pursuit of the red dot enemy.

It took a while to adjust to the three dogs and other felines. They all had unique personalities, various health and behavioral issues and rescue stories of their own. All the dogs were from South Carolina, two also from death row and one rescued off the streets. All the cats were older than me. I was the youngest in the house.

I didn't get to spend all my time with the other cats and dogs. I only came up for supervised visits at first, because I liked to pounce on the cats, scare the dogs, or whap the humans as they walked by. But one day, as the flowers bloomed full and beautiful, and iridescent hummingbirds began to appear at the feeders, I received the okay to move into the main house for good. I was even given permission to sleep in the real bed.

I still felt fearful at times. If someone moved during the night and woke me from my sleep I would lash out and hiss. A few times I even hurt the humans and that made me feel awful inside. I vowed to keep working on the lessons that She-Fe had so compassionately instilled in me. I worked on being grounded and in the moment. On being focused but also carefree. I knew many of my behaviors were in response to the past and that any negative behavior could easily be made into a positive. I thought of She-Fe's reminder: *Don't be so quick to discard parts of you because you see them as negative. You may need to rely on those parts someday to do something positive.* I smiled, thinking of him. *Focus on less fear and more peace.*

The human kept her promise and never gave up on me. One day she came home from Dr. Wu's place and told me she had wonderful news. Dr. Wu wanted a virtual mascot who represented his teachings. She'd told him about me, and he'd jumped at the chance to have me represent the Wu Healing Center. I couldn't believe my ears. She-Fe would be so proud of me! The human must have recognized my happiness and I let her lift me up and hug me. I ran through the house telling any animal companion I could find the great news. I'd come a long way from the street cat that people held in disdain. I was a healing cat now, about to spread the

Wu Kitty: Rescued From The Row

message of love, resilience and living in the now. I had wisdom to share and a story to tell. This was part of my purpose.

And I was a hit in my new role! Everyone at the Wu Healing Center knew about me and I developed a social media following. I branched out to include my own personal Facebook page, "Wu Kitty ~ Wisdom in the 'Me~now,'" where I could share my insights, the daily news of my fellow rescue mates and all the wonderful things going on over at Dr. Wu's centers. Everything had come full circle. She-Fe's wisdom had provided a foundation, not only to help me survive on the streets and the horrible circumstances at the ACC, but to continue to grow each day with my new family and help others by sharing my newfound wisdom. My story did matter. I mattered! My human realized it, Dr. Wu and his people realized it, my Facebook followers realized it, and finally I did too.

Two Years Later

I arrived at my home in April 2013. By 2015 my life was amazing. I celebrated birthdays and holidays with my family. I wrote posts for Facebook and posed for photos for Instagram and Pinterest. I practiced qigong and continued to apply the Tao to my life. I had friends and food and warmth.

But every now and then, I thought about my former street pals. I had faith She-Fe was doing well and helping others just like me. I knew this because sometimes during deep meditation or at night when I was lost in a dream state he would come to me. I didn't spend a lot of time thinking about what may have happened to my former cellmates at the ACC. I knew the statistics of what happens to animals in kill shelters.

But I always wondered what happened to my pitty pal Momo, who shared pizza with me in those dirty alleys. I hoped he'd managed to elude capture and avoid the sad fate that befell so many dogs like him in New York.

One day, a friend stopped by. He was a frequent visitor and we all loved him. He played with us and didn't get mad if I accidentally bit or scratched him, or burst into one of my hissy cat fits that I still have some mornings. This particular day, I heard him say that he'd rescued a dog from New York City. My ears perked up. There were a lot of dogs in New York City, but I had that sliver of hope....

"He's a sweetheart," he said. "He's afraid of cars and flashing lights. He's awesome. I named him Momo. It just came to me when I saw him. Anyway, here's his picture."

He held up his iPhone. I casually jumped up on the couch and took a look at the photo the humans were admiring, and my heart almost stopped. Unless my eyes played tricks on me, I was looking at a larger, grown-up version of my pizza-eating pal! I could hardly believe it. I blinked and looked again, just in case. The picture remained the same, and my heart swelled with happiness. Not only was he safe, he lived in the same state as me!

I rubbed up against our friend's arm and gave him several head butts, trying to convey my gratitude.

Wu Kitty: Rescued From The Row

"Hey, did you see that?" he asked, surprised. "Wu's loving on me. Who knew?" Everyone laughed and I purred loudly.

In the now. That is where it's at, friends. Live in the present. Know that you are meant for great things. You have a purpose and no one can fulfill it but you. Shake off those labels. Hold your head high like a tigress and just be. Take it from me, Wu Kitty — it can and will end well.

Belladonna: Sweet Sugar Kitty

I'm a very special kitty. In fact, I'm so special I was adopted twice! I know what you're saying: How on earth did that happen? Well, let me tell you my story.

My first mama met me at the shelter when I was still a pretty tiny little thing, and naturally, she fell in love with me. What's not to love about a gorgeous, sleek black kitten with golden-green eyes who loves to play and goof around, right? I picked up toys and threw them in the air and chased after them and made her laugh. Then when she stroked me, I turned up the adorable one more notch and started purring like crazy.

After all my efforts to win her over, I wasn't the least bit surprised when First Mama picked me out of the kitten room and took me home to First Daddy.

And guess what? I was their First Kitten, too!

Belladonna: Sweet Sugar Kitty

I had many happy times with First Mama and First Daddy. They played with me and loved me right to pieces, and I felt absolutely adored — as well I should have.

But then something strange happened. I started feeling kind of weird and I was hungry all the time. First Mama and First Daddy thought it was normal for a growing kitten to be hungry, so they fed me as much as I could eat and they didn't get too mad when I started licking their cooking pans and stuff. It wasn't until I started playing less and less that they started to get worried. When First Mama picked me up and noticed how skinny I'd gotten, she took me straight to the vet. And wouldn't you know it, that mean old vet stole some of my blood and pee and ran a bunch of tests.

I settled on First Mama's lap to wait patiently for the test results, When the vet returned, she looked very serious.

"First Mama," the vet said, "it looks like your little Belladonna has diabetes."

"What does that mean?" First Mama said. "Is Bella going to be okay?"

"It's very rare to find diabetes in kittens," said the vet. "And it's going to be a bit of a lifestyle change for you. Diabetic cats need to have daily insulin shots, and they have to eat special food so they won't get sicker."

"Oh no," said First Mama.

The vet sat down next to First Mama and gave me a pat on the head. I looked up at her with my best Adorable Kitten look. "I'm not going to lie to you," she told First Mama. "It's hard to get diabetes under control at

Rescued Volume 2

first because we have to figure out how much insulin she needs in order to keep her blood glucose normal. We'll probably have to do that here at the hospital for a few days, or we may need to send her down to the specialists in Portland."

"How much is that going to cost?" asked First Mama.

"I'd guess in the range of several hundred to a thousand dollars. But I can't be sure how much the specialist will charge."

"Oh gosh, I can't afford that," First Mama said with tears in her eyes. "And is it even fair to…you know…."

"I wish I could answer that question for you," said the vet.

"Maybe I should have her put to sleep."

"Hey, wait!" I said. "You don't need to put me to sleep. I can go to sleep all by myself, see?" I curled up in her lap in a tight little ball, gave a purry little sigh and closed my eyes. I felt First Mama's tears drip onto my fur.

"She's just a kitten. It's not fair!" cried First Mama.

"With proper management of her disease, Belladonna could have a very good life," said the vet.

"But I can't do that. What can I do?" First Mama asked.

"I can call around to the shelters and see if there's one that will take her," the vet said.

"I adopted her from the shelter in Bath," said First Mama. She sniffled and said, "They told me they'd take her back if I couldn't care for her anymore. But I feel so bad. I really do love her."

"Of course you do," the vet told First Mama. "You've already done a lot more than many people would.

Belladonna: Sweet Sugar Kitty

Sometimes the most courageous and loving thing you can do is give your kitty a second chance."

"Will you make the calls? I just…I don't think I can do it," First Mama stammered.

"Of course I will. Do you want to leave her here with us or do you want to take some time to say goodbye first?"

"Maybe I should leave her here with you. At least she can start getting healthier that way."

First Mama picked me up and gave me a big kiss. I could see her eyes glistening with tears as she petted me in all my favorite places.

That was the last time I saw First Mama.

As I waited in my cage at the vet's office, I could hear her making the calls.

The first call she made was to the shelter where First Mama had adopted me. "You don't have the facilities to care for a diabetic cat? I understand. But there are other places that can do it? Okay, I'll try HART and Cumberland County. Thanks!"

Then she got on the phone and had a long talk with somebody else. I couldn't hear the other end of the conversation because of all the meowing and barking and talking, but I knew it was good news because she said, "Wonderful! I'll bring her down on Saturday."

And that's how I ended up at HART of Maine in a room with eight other diabetic cats.

I was starting to feel better since I'd been getting some insulin, so I was all ready to climb and play and have fun with the other kitties. I started tossing toys around and running up and down the cat carriers, and this one big blue-eyed tabby guy glared at me.

"Hi, I'm Belladonna!" I said, trotting up to him with my tail held high.

"Go away," he said.

"Why are you being such a grumpy-pants?" I asked. "I just want to be your friend!"

"I don't want to be anybody's friend," he said. "I hate it here. I want my mama back."

"Don't mind him," said another black cat from across the room, "He's just getting used to the place. My name's Denny, by the way. What's yours?"

"I'm Belladonna. But people call me Bella for short. Do you want to play?"

After a couple of weeks of getting insulin shots and eating this stuff the humans called fancy feasts or something like that, I started feeling a lot better! I wasn't a big fan of having my ears poked and getting shots every day, but I did the best I could to be a good girl and take my medicine. This one lady, Margaret, was the chief caretaker for all of us diabetic cats. She knew how to do ear pokes and give shots, and she showed some other people at the shelter how to do it, too.

Then, one morning about a month after I'd arrived at HART, Margaret poked my ear and put a drop of my blood on the test strip. After it beeped, she said, "Bella, your blood glucose is only 85. I think you might be going into remission! I'm going to have the other volunteers keep testing you to be sure, and I'm going to call the vet and have them do a curve. But I think you might not need to have any more insulin shots."

That was great news for sure. I knew I was getting stronger: I felt better than I had in a long time.

Belladonna: Sweet Sugar Kitty

I enjoyed myself as much as I could at the shelter, but I lived in a small room and most of the cats there were a lot older than me. Christmas came and went and nobody brought me home. I started to believe that maybe I should give up thinking anyone would want me.

But then one day, I heard some voices in the hallway. One of them I had never heard before. She was saying something about being interested in volunteering, and that she was here for a tour. The shelter person showed her the various rooms and explained what they do at HART of Maine — that every single person who works there is a volunteer, so volunteers are *really* important. I could hear the new voice sounding more and more excited about working with us kitties.

They stopped in the kitchen and the shelter person showed the new person where they prepared foods and medicines. I overheard the new person say, "I've always had a special place in my heart for black cats."

The shelter person said, "We've got three of them in the diabetic room. You should go in and take a look."

Well, I started grooming my fur and washing my face as soon as I heard that! I wanted to look my best when the new person came in to meet me. I pawed at the little shaved spot on my neck where the vet had drawn blood for the glucose curve that proved my remission. I hoped it wouldn't bother this new person.

Denny gave himself a quick wash, too, but Angus, the other black cat, was still sound asleep. He was pretty old, so I guess he needed the extra rest.

Then the door opened, and there she was: The new person! She was all wrapped up in extra clothes because it was so cold outside, and her blue wool hat looked like it would be really fun and soft to knead.

It was love at first sight for me. I ran across the tops of the cages and hopped onto a cat tree so I could rub against her hands and bonk her and purr all over her. "You're my mama!" I said.

"Who are you, little one?" she asked as her fingers stroked my cheeks and under my chin.

I purred and purred!

"That's Bella," the shelter person said. "She's actually been in remission for a little while."

"So she doesn't need insulin right now?" the new person asked as I rubbed my cheek across her face. I climbed back onto the cat tower, and the new person reached toward me and started stroking my head and shoulders. I purred even louder.

"Oh man," the new person said, "this little Bella sure is a love, and I think I'm falling in love, too."

"Might you be interested in adopting her?" the shelter person asked.

"Well, I have to talk to my other cats first," she said. "We did lose two cats pretty recently, and I want to make sure they're doing all right before I bring in another cat."

"What happened to the other cats?" the shelter person asked.

"Dahlia died from lymphoma," the new person said, "and Kissy had one of those weird one-in-a-million anesthesia reactions...."

I could feel how sad she was.

"I'll make you happy again!" I said, and I climbed onto her shoulder and licked her ear.

Belladonna: Sweet Sugar Kitty

"Oh God, I'm a sucker," the new person said.

I guess my charm and charisma must have worked because the very next week, the new person was back at the shelter with Margaret, learning how to poke my ears and give me my shots. (I'd gone out of remission again — phooey!). The week after that, she came into the diabetic room after her volunteer shift, holding a very pretty purple kitty carrier. As soon as she unzipped the door to the carrier, I ran inside as fast as I could meowing, "Mama, I'm ready to go home!"

"I guess she's ready to go home," the shelter person said.

Of course I am! That's what I just said! Don't these humans understand anything? I thought.

"I guess so!" said Mama (as soon as she showed up with the carrier I decided to call her Mama, not new person). She zipped the carrier closed and brought me out to her car. Snow was falling but I was warm and cozy. As we headed back to her home, I curled up happily as the music played and the windshield wipers thump-squeaked the snow away.

"You've already won me over, in spite of me," Mama sang. And I purred right along.

Once we got to Mama's house, I smelled two other cats, but Mama wouldn't let me meet them. She placed me in the front room and closed the French doors behind her before I could get out of the carrier. But I could see those other cats through the glass panes and I wanted to say hi!

I scratched at the door as Mama did some chores. Then when she came back in, I ran between her legs and out of the room.

"Hi! I'm a kitten!" I said.

"Awwwww," the tabby and white cat said.

The black cat sighed and said, "Oh, I suppose."

I went right up and touched noses with the tabby and white cat.

"I'm Thomas," he said. "Want to be friends?"

"Oh yes, of course! And my name's Belladonna. But you can call me Bella if you want."

"How about you? Do you want to be friends?" I said, trotting up to the black cat.

She hissed at me and I jumped back.

"Don't worry about Siouxsie," Thomas said. "She's just grumpy because her hips hurt. Here, let's have a snuggle before dinner."

He led me to the most delightful bed I've ever seen: It was big and soft and had nice, high sides. I let Thomas make himself comfortable first, and then I climbed in next to him. That was the best nap I'd had since I was a little baby in the nest with my brothers and sisters.

Later on I woke up to the sound of Mama puttering around the kitchen and I smelled something super

Belladonna: Sweet Sugar Kitty

delicious. Thomas got out of the bed too and hopped onto the counter to investigate.

"Thomas," Mama said, "you're delaying dinner for everyone."

Siouxsie grumped and then she jumped on the counter, too.

"Siouxsie!" Mama said. "You're old enough to know better. Besides, I've got something I need to do before you eat. Bella, come here."

I hopped onto the butcher block across from the counter, where Mama had my special kit out for me. The first thing she did was poke a little hole in my ear — and trust me when I tell you she wasn't very good at it! It took her at least four tries before she poked me the way she needed to. Phooey! But I tried to be a good kitty and sit still while she put a little drop of my blood on a testing strip and read the number. Then after that she gave me my shot. Phooey again! But I was used to the routine and knew I had to have shots before I ate to stay healthy, so I was a good girl and let Mama give me my medicine.

Then we all got to eat, and oh my Bast, Mama served the most delicious gooshy foods I'd ever had! I ate all my supper lickety split, but I was still hungry so I asked Thomas and Siouxsie if I could have some of theirs. They didn't answer, so I just took that as a yes and nudged Siouxsie away from her dish.

"Belladonna Moonshadow Kelley," Mama snapped. "Get away from Siouxsie's food!"

Then she picked me up and put me in the human litter box room and closed the door behind me. I scratched and scratched, but I couldn't get out. Finally, after what seemed like forever, Mama opened the door. I ran to Thomas's and Siouxsie's dishes to see if they'd left anything for me. They hadn't, and that made me sad, so I curled up in a kitty bed on the couch with a sigh.

Things went on this way, with me getting my shots before breakfast and supper and then getting locked in the bathroom to eat so I wouldn't steal Thomas's and Siouxsie's food. After about a week, Mama took me to her vet, Dr. Alden, who said this was the first time she'd ever seen a healthy diabetic kitten.

"There is one very small study on kittens with diabetes that shows they were born with a pancreas that's too small to produce enough insulin," Dr. Alden said, "but this little one is way too healthy to have that problem."

"I'm testing her blood glucose at home, and she's getting raw food just like Thomas and Siouxsie," Mama said.

"It's delicious, too!" I purred.

"You adopted her from HART?" Dr. Alden asked. "I actually sent a diabetic kitty there myself a while ago. The owner couldn't take care of him, unfortunately."

"Oh, who is it?" I meowed. "I'm dying to know! Pleeeease tell me!"

"Oh my gosh, she's got the sweetest little chirp," Dr. Alden said as I rubbed my head against her hand. "Well, Bella, let's get you checked out."

She opened my mouth and looked at my beautiful teeth, and then she put her stethoscope against my chest — brrrr! "Her heart and lungs sound great," said Dr. Alden.

Belladonna: Sweet Sugar Kitty

As she squeezed my belly and sides, Dr. Alden said, "It looks like you're doing a wonderful job with her so far. Keep up the good work! And if you have any questions about diabetes, please don't hesitate to ask. I'm delighted you adopted her because adopting a cat with special needs is not an easy choice to make."

"I fell in love," Mama said. "What else could I do? Besides, I know I can handle her care, both medically and financially, so I'm grateful for that, too. All kitties deserve forever homes."

With a purr, I collapsed into Mama's arms. Then Dr. Alden picked me back up and stuck a thermometer in my butt! Yuck! "Maybe I don't like you so much after all, Dr. Alden!" I meowed.

"Sorry, baby, it's got to be done," she said.

The thermometer beeped and Dr. Alden looked at the number. "Her temperature's normal.

"It looks like aside from the diabetes, your Bella is a very healthy kitty. Congratulations! I'll tell you what: I'm going to read up on kittens with diabetes to see if there's anything else I need to know in order to keep her healthy, too."

"Thanks, Dr. Alden, you're awesome as usual. I'll be bringing Thomas in for his dental in a couple of weeks, so I'll see you then."

About a week later, I was just doing my normal goofy thing, but a few hours after I got my shot, I started feeling super-dizzy and hungry. I was so famished I tried to eat everything I could get my teeth on, even cardboard! Mama saw me gnawing on a shipping box and realized what was happening. She'd learned enough about working with diabetic kitties, thanks to Margaret, that she knew she needed to test my blood sugar. After a brief struggle, I let Mama poke my ear.

"Oh, dear," she said when she read the number on the testing machine. She fed me some nasty, super-sweet stuff and I started feeling better.

Then Mama called Margaret and said, "Yeah, she went hypo on one unit. Her blood glucose was down to 45. Do you think I should go down to half a unit twice a day? Uh-huh; yeah, okay, I'll do that and call the vet first thing tomorrow."

Mama was true to her word and called Dr. Alden to tell her what had happened. "I think I want to do a BG curve this weekend," Mama said. "Yes, I got the instructions from FelineDiabetes.com. Every two hours for 12 hours…yes, I'll email you the results and you can let me know what you think."

And wouldn't you know it? She did! She poked my poor little ears every two hours to take a reading of my blood glucose. But Mama was very happy with the numbers she got, and so was Dr. Alden, who told Mama to bring me down to half a unit of insulin, once a day.

It turned out even that was too much, because I was in remission again! Hooray! No more ear pokes, no more shots, none of that!

Okay, I'm getting ahead of myself. I did get more ear pokes for a while because Mama wanted to make sure I was actually in remission. (She still pokes my ears once in a while, even though it's been three years since I needed an insulin shot — phooey!)

Belladonna: Sweet Sugar Kitty

And guess what was the coolest thing of all? Mama, Thomas and Siouxsie write a blog called Paws and Effect that includes a weekly advice column, and they let me write it with them! Who knew a little shelter kitty like me would someday get to be a world-famous feline author? At first I thought it was super-fun because I got to talk about how beautiful I was, but Siouxsie grumped at me when I marveled at my lovely fur and delightfully long tail instead of helping readers. What did she expect? I was still just a kitten and I hadn't accumulated nearly as much wisdom as she and Thomas had, so I figured I could at least make people laugh until I learned everything I could from my feline housemates.

To my great surprise, none of their advice involved giving cats treats whenever we ask for them, or avoiding trips to the vet. In fact, if anything, Thomas and Siouxsie were always telling people to take their cats to the vet for checkups and if they were worried about their kitty's behavior. I don't know why, since they both hated going to the vet.

"Aren't you supposed to be telling humans to give their cats whatever they want?" I asked Thomas one day. "After all, you're giving advice about cats to people, and they need to know that they should always do what we think they should do."

"Well, now, sweetie, that's not always true," Thomas said and gave me a quick lick on the ear.

"Tee hee hee, that tickles!" I said. "Why not?"

"There are lots of things we cats don't like, but as we get older, we learn that at times we just have to let the humans believe we're doing what they want, like going to the vet or letting them vacuum the house."

"I suppose you're right. It's kind of like I made Mama think I was doing what she wanted when she poked my ears and gave me shots, but she was really doing what I wanted because I wanted to feel better and I was making sure I trained her to help me do that."

"Absolutely," Thomas said. "Now, let's curl up and go to sleep.

As I grew up, I learned more about human behavior and how it affects cats, so I was able to share my own tips about what humans should do to make life as good as possible for their cats. One day I asked Mama if she'd be willing to do something with our blog to help the other diabetic kitties at the shelter to find homes. We talked it over and came up with a feature called Sugar Kitty Wednesday, in which she highlighted a cat from HART of Maine's diabetic cat room every week. She interviewed the cats and shared their stories on Paws and Effect, and I'm sure that did a lot to help several of my diabetic friends found homes over the next couple of months. After all, as I've said before, I'm a very special kitty and everything I do is magical!

It wasn't just Mama making me feel better. I was making her feel better, too. You see, Mama was so very sad after losing her Dahlia and Kissy so close together that for a while there I was worried she'd never be happy again. I decided I had to do something about that! Every day I'd run around playing with one of my toys: I'd chase it all over the house and then run up and down my cat tree yelling "Mrrow?

Belladonna: Sweet Sugar Kitty

Rrrow! Grrrreeep?!?" and it made Mama laugh and smile every time.

Eventually Mama stopped being sad all the time. Again, I'm sure that had everything to do with me, although she still remembered Dahlia and Kissy with a smile and a tear.

Even though I've stayed in remission, Mama has continued to do her best to help people learn about feline diabetes and how it's not a death sentence and not nearly as scary as it seems at first. She wrote a bunch of posts on our blog and on Catster about diabetes in order to encourage people to keep their "sugar kitties," as she called them.

One cool thing that happened because of my diabetes is that Mama learned about a great organization called Diabetic Cats In Need. They help people who have diabetic cats with education and financial assistance. In fact, they even provided the blood glucose testing kit and supplies that Mama got from the shelter when she adopted me. Mama was so impressed by their work that she wrote a whole article about them for Catster and started following them on Facebook so she could keep up with them and make donations when she could.

One day just a few months after I adopted Mama, something really weird started happening. Mama started putting things in boxes and throwing things out and giving things away. I heard her say we were moving to See Addel, but I didn't know what that was. It wasn't until one early morning when Mama put all three of us in our carriers and plunked us in the back seat of her car that I realized just what moving to See Addel meant.

We spent tons and tons of time in the car, but every night we stopped at a hotel so we got to sleep in the bed with Mama. Thomas and I had some fun with her because we'd try to hide where she couldn't find us when it was time to leave every morning. But somehow, she always did manage to track us down. I'm glad she did because I'd hate to have been left somewhere between Maine and See Addel!

When we finally got there, I found out that See Addel was actually Seattle, and it was really pretty. And Mama's sister was there to greet us, and there were sun puddles and everything! Thomas and I both curled up in the big sun puddle on Mama's bed, and Siouxsie grumped at us for stealing all the warm spots. We decided to be nice and share our sun puddle with her; after all, she was an old lady-cat and we're nice, respectful kitties.

Mama was ever so much happier here in Seattle than she ever was in Maine. She said she'd found her kindred spirits. I guess that's kinda like what happened to me when I met Thomas, because we're snuggle buddies for life now!

After we'd been living in Seattle for a while, Mama read on Facebook that Diabetic Cats In Need was looking for volunteers to help them with a bunch of different things, including something that Mama is very, very good at: social media and website magic. Mama was so grateful for everything DCIN had done for me and for lots of other sugar kitties that she decided she'd apply to be their secretary and social media manager.

BELLADONNA: SWEET SUGAR KITTY

Mama's been working with DCIN for about a year now. She makes special graphics for their Facebook page, and she's building them a whole new website, dcin.info, so they can do even more to help sugar kitties like me stay in their homes and get the medical attention they need. If it hadn't been for DCIN, I might not have had the chance to live this amazing and joyful life. I'm so grateful to everyone who helped me, from First Mama to First Mama's vet, to DCIN and HART of Maine — and, of course, Mama! I'm so glad Mama and I were able to heal each other because now we're both unstoppable!

THE STORY OF LITTLE PIP

The little girl comes to me first. Through the cage I see her large blue-green eyes behind purple-framed glasses. She is a young one, five years old, with a laugh that is boisterous, filling my heart, making me purr. Then the mother comes. She has her arms crossed as she leans in to see me. They both put their fingers into the cage, pet me on the chin. I hold up my left paw, the one that has been damaged for good. They say I am reaching out, maybe I am. The mother walks away. I watch as she looks into each cage in the room. There are fifty-two of us waiting. The little girl has made the rounds several times, only she keeps coming back to me. My short fur is the type of gray so deep that it looks blue. My green eyes are rare, say the people who bring my food. I think the visitors who come into the room don't see me. Maybe I blend into

The Story of Little Pip

the gray cage. Perhaps I am dirty to them. Gray and dirty from the gutter. They move toward the patterned cats always. Black and white patches, orange stripes. Long, fluffy fur. Yellow eyes, so many yellow eyes. The little girl and her mother are the first.

I continue to watch the mother. The little girl moves toward the three kittens below me. They are peeping out sounds that make her laugh. The precious laugh that I refuse to let escape my heart. I see these two humans have brought gifts for all of us. A large box full of cotton mice, feathers on miniature poles with strings, the little pebbles that I must now dig into when I need to relieve myself. Cans of tuna, of which I know I will be given very little because there are so many of us. Too many.

We know when it is time. We feel the electric fear in the air, the private motif of despair. When they take one or several to the room, we, the rest of the cats, stare into one another's eyes. We want the people to know that we know, that we understand we will never again see the cats they are taking and we hope that it is fast and painless. After the cats taken to the room are concluded, the rest of us stay silent for a long time.

I have been here one month. I know that cats are concluded after two months. The people who feed us and clean our cages won't speak of it. They want to cuddle and swoon but on the day cats leave for conclusion it feels like false compassion. It is a requisite performance.

The little girl comes to me again. The mother continues to look at all of the other cats, but finally, she comes to me as well. I have a small voice, I am a small cat even though I am fully-grown. Young at one year and three months, but I know things from living in the wild. I know how to spring in zigzags to ditch the coyotes. I know the raccoons will leave me alone if I leave them with something delicious. The dogs are on leashes more often than not. I have managed to escape the talons of falcons and great horned owls. Yes, am clever, but my petite size and my gray color have given me leverage. My meows are almost half-meows, I do not whine, I trill my voice. The mother comments on my blue nose. Yes, I am trying to tell her, I am a good one. The others are good as well, but I am a better one.

The mother tells the little girl to say good-bye. They both scratch my chin once more, and they leave. They, too, must think I am from the gutter. It is cold in the room, cement floors dip down to a center drain. The people who feed us hose down the floor. There is one window, only there is nothing to see but sky. I miss that sky, starlings flying in formation, putting me into a trance. I want to leap high and grab those perfect beings. They might quiver in my mouth and I would hold them down and make them go in a quiet peace. Sometimes I see ravens through that small window. They are loud and I see their brains working behind their eyes. But I am here, and they are there, and I want them to see that I, too, have a brain working behind my green eyes.

I wait for the mother and the little girl to return the next day, but they do not. I sleep. I curl as tight as I can because I think that if I twist into myself enough, I will be warm. This is how I did it outside. Many people

The Story of Little Pip

come into the cold room, many people overlook me. They want the full, fringed ones. I want to tell them that I have much to offer. They do not want a small one, maybe they think that I am frail. I want to tell them about me defeating the fox. Her red hair brushing back from her sleek body, her kits crying in the distance. She and I held our gaze. I could see that she would do anything to take me to those babies. I darted and ran and I could hear her running fast behind me, I could smell her musk. I saw the road and scurried across because I knew I could flow through those cars. I did this, I puzzled the slick beast and I won. Her babies cried.

Almost two weeks later, the mother and the little girl return. I let them know that I am still here, but they know. They come straight to me, put their fingers into my cage while my damaged paw hangs in front of me. When I stand, I look normal, when I walk, I walk like nothing happened. I know I can fool anyone about this paw. They don't have to understand the crushing, I have already let the memory move out of me, no use to me now. I move forward in my head like I stalk all tiny creatures in the tall grasses.

The mother leaves the room and speaks to the people at the front desk. The little girl stays. She speaks to the adults in the room, the people who feed me and the people who visit but ignore me. I see the mother sitting in the other room. The little girl goes to her, then comes back to me. She repeats this pattern many times. A woman who always sits at the front desk comes to take me out of the cage. She carries me, only I no longer see the little girl and the mother. I think she may be taking me to my conclusion. I think I have to let go now. I am small, but I will not let the bigger cats see my fear. All those chases at night with coyotes yipping at each other to corner me, that fear was nothing compared to what I feel in this moment.

Then the woman turns another way and takes me into a confined room. The mother and the little girl are there. A basket of toys sits on the floor, smelling of other cats, smelling of this room. The mother sits with her chin resting on her fist, elbow resting on knee. I see she has a brain behind those hazel eyes. She is watching the little girl. She is watching me. I go to the mother and she is gentle. I jump into her lap, she knows how to keep it light enough, she knows how to avoid smothering me. The little girl is delighted, she dumps all of the toys from the basket onto the floor and shakes them at me. The mother explains that she must sit down in a chair and be calm. The little girl does this so I go to her, I stand on my hind legs, put my front paws on her knees and then I hear that laugh. I purr. I leap into her lap. I see the mother smile. I am good in their energy. I can see the mother's aura, I can see all of the colors. I can see me with her and I will fall into this little girl's happiness because it is contagious.

The woman who works at the front comes into the room and takes me away. She takes me to the cold room, she puts me into the cage and I know, they have put me back into the gutter. I close my eyes and try to forget the mother and the little girl. I am letting the dreams come into my head, letting the closeness out, not holding onto it because if I do, it will hurt me.

The Story of Little Pip

A sharp clanking wakes me. The woman from the front takes me once again, she places me inside a cardboard box and closes the lid that forms into a handle. She carries me as I try to see out of the tiny holes that spread across the top of each side. She places the box down onto the ground and I see the mother. I hear the woman ask the mother if she wants to change my name, but she tells them, no, that she and the little girl love my name. Pippa. She picks up the box. She and the little girl take me outside, put me in a car, and I hear the engine. It frightens me, makes me feel like I can't grab onto something solid so I cry out. The mother talks to me, she soothes me, the little girl echoes everything the mother says. I don't know where they are taking me. Perhaps they will release me into the open, into the mouths of large creatures that hunt me.

We are in the car for a long time, then I hear the engine stop and the mother carries the box into a house. She carries me upstairs and I hear dogs barking. I can't tell how many are here, I smell dog odor everywhere. The mother places the box onto carpet and opens it. I vault and see that I am in a bedroom. The walls are blue like water. There is a large window and I spring onto the desk beneath it so that I can see outside, I can evaluate where I am. I see open space, I see areas where elk have grazed, I can see the flat grass where they once laid.

There is a bowl of food and a bowl of water. There is a people bed that I jump onto. The mother and little girl are patient with me. They let me walk the room, take in every corner. I see the box with the little pebbles. I hear the dogs barking. I think it is uncomplicated here, I have no problems. I lay down and they can see that I have no concern. Those dogs can't scare me.

While I am staying in this room, the mother comes in at night, sits on the bed, and taps her fingers on a laptop. I purr and curl up next to the mother. She pets me and talks to me in a soft voice. I hear a man's voice often. He comes in to see me. He is the father. He is loud. He tries to be gentle with me, only I can tell he has never before been around a cat. The little girl comes into the room often during the days. She is loud as well. She holds the thin pole with the feathers hanging on a string and I like it. I stalk it. She laughs hard and I bat at the makeshift bird, I cackle and pretend it's real. This makes the little girl laugh harder. The mother often sits on the floor and watches us play. She comments on how I won't jump high. She says she thinks something must have happened to my front paw. I walk better in front of her. I don't want her to think I am flawed. She might take me back to the cold place if she thinks I am not right.

The Story of Little Pip

The mother is bringing in my food, I hear the dogs out in the hallway, then they push in. They are huge, massive, I am tiny. They see me and both lunge so I turn to face them and I hiss like the big cats, hold up my claws to show them that I can scratch their eyes out. The mother grabs one, the father grabs the other and they yank the big dogs out. The dogs are also gray, but not blue like me, they are silver. One with a short tail, one with a long tail.

They keep me in the room, alone, for two weeks. The mother and little girl continue to visit me many times during the day, to bring my food, to clean my box with pebbles. The mother continues to come each night. I am relaxed. I know they won't let those big dogs in. They take me out of the room and let me explore the entire house except for one room. It is the mother's room and I can hear the dogs behind the door. I know they are in cages, I hear the clinking of paws against metal, and then they are calm. I walk through the house, the rooms with large windows, I see the couches, I see the dogs' bowls, I see the doors made of glass, showing me the outside. I sit and I wait for them to open the door, to let me lunge at the red finches in the tall weeping willow hanging over the deck. They do not open the door. I see the scratching post near a couch. I leap onto the kitchen counter where I wait for them to turn on the water faucet so that I may drink. They think I don't know what these things are, the things that make up a home. I wait by the door again, only they won't open the door, they won't let me go outside. After a while, they put me back into my room and I hear the dogs roaming the house.

Rescued Volume 2

A few days later, the mother takes me into her bedroom. I see the dogs in their cages. The one with the short tail is whimpering, I see that she is a female. The one with the long tail is a male. He lays in a quiet stare, fixated on me as I explore the room. I don't know which dog I can trust more. They have never been around a cat before, I can tell by the way they reveal their lack of wisdom. Their surprise, their smelling of me. The female begins to bark so the mother squirts her with a squirt bottle, but she continues. The mother commands her to sit, and she obeys and stops barking. The mother tosses a biscuit into her cage. The dog gulps it without taking her eyes off me. I decide to go past the other dog because he is not barking, he is calm. Only when I pass, a fear erupts in him and he lunges at me with snarls. The bars hold him back, the mother squirts him and he cowers. I perceive that he has been somewhere else, I sense his pain from a previous place, I recognize that the mother saved him. I know he will never bother me again.

The mother does this for about a week. She takes me to the room, she tosses biscuits into the cages whenever the dogs remain calm as I saunter past. Then one day she lets me out of my room to walk the house and I see the male is there. I can hear the female barking in the cage upstairs. But the male is out like me. He avoids eye contact. When I walk near him, he leaves and moves into a different room. The mother gives him biscuits if he takes a chance and glances my way.

The mother is trying to give me wet food. I eat the dry food, but she can't work out why I won't eat the wet. She tries several different types. Chicken, turkey,

The Story of Little Pip

tuna, salmon, herring, duck. She tries loafs and chunks and bits with gravy. I feel bad for her. It is not fresh, no matter how long it has been sealed in that can. The dry is like many scraps I have eaten. I finally eat the wet, not because I like it, but because I know it is important for her to see me finish. She pets me often. She continues to come to my room at night. After a while, she lets me sleep with the little girl whenever she naps. Each day, the mother tucks the little girl into her bed and reads her books. I now understand that there is something different about this little girl. She is not like the typicals. She has an aura of illness only she doesn't understand that she is ill. I can sense that behind those big blue-green eyes there are masses in her brain. Two complex masses that stretch to the back of her skull. After the mother finishes reading books, she sings the same song about sunshine to the little girl while she uses her hands to do small, short squeezes on her legs. I like the squeezes so I knead the blankets whenever she does this. I am synchronized with the mother as we press into plush. I purr. This mother knows how to make us move into sleep.

 As the little girl slumbers, I inch up and nap next to her, leaning most of my body onto her chest. I feel her breaths, I feel her dreaming and I like what she sees. I cannot know, but I feel that she has bright images moving in her head, moving around the masses like they don't exist. When she wakes, I follow her because I know the female dog is in the cage and cannot get to me.

 When I am in my room, the female dog never leaves the other side of the door. She lies down close and I lie down close, this barrier between us. She places her large, pinkish nose near the bottom of the door. I put my paw under the door, I try to reach her. I can feel the vibrations of her short tail wagging. We smell one another through the door always. At night, the dogs sleep in the mother's room. At night, the little girl sleeps in the mother's bed and the father sleeps in my room. It is the illness I think. The nights are long and I think the mother needs to believe the little girl is tranquil, the masses unchanged.

The mother begins to make comments about me to the father and the little girl. She says she doesn't think I was a stray like the people at the cold place told her. She says they may think I was a stray but that I know my way around a house too much. She knows and I think it is okay she knows. She will not make me leave like the others did. She will not push me out and never let me back in. There is no need for her to be aware of the details. I have forgotten. She does not need to understand the truth about my front paw. I see that she thinks I am exquisite, and not from the gutter, even if I did spend some time scavenging after the others pushed me out. I will not think of the others ever again. I give this gift to the mother. I make her understand that I am in the right place.

Sometimes, when I am out of my room, the mother brings down the female dog on a leash. She lets her come close to me and she throws her bits of turkey. I can tell it is a special treat because the dog never turned away from me when the mother gave her normal biscuits. But this is something with extra goodness. This

The Story of Little Pip

is something that makes the female turn away from me. The mother does this over many days. She finally gets the female to lie down. She is on the leash, but she will lie down and focus on the mother now instead of me. The mother gives her the turkey bits. I want some of the turkey bits. The male dog wants some, too. So we linger, we try to get the bits the mother throws to the female. So the mother throws us tiny bits as well.

After two months from the first time I arrived in this home, the mother lets out the female dog without a leash. She is excited, she wags her tail a lot. She follows me and at first I think it is okay, but then she is in my space. She will not walk away like the male, she wants to be close, she wants to smell me when I jump onto the kitchen counter, when I jump off, when I go underneath the kitchen chair, when I want to sit in front of the doors of glass, when I leap onto the couch. This dog is annoying me. The mother sees this, she follows us from a distance. She watches. She has the turkey bits.

The female is eager, her short tail is wagging like the fluttering wings of those butterflies I once chased. I am measuring the dog's energy. She is not agitated like the first day I came, instead, she understands that I am the one behind the door for so long. My paw to her nose, her nose to my nose. I know she is no longer a threat. I walk the rooms, she follows. Only, she is too close. She is so close that when she puts her nose to me, she pushes me with her strength. I walk faster. She walks faster. The mother follows us, watching. The male dog watches the female dog. He is below her in stature, he does what she tells him to do. But this female is tricky, not like other dogs. She is subtle, it is hard sometimes to read the cues. But the male dog has it down. She looks at him and he knows how he is to behave. There is no growling or biting, he hears her silent talk. I must watch the female closer. She thinks she is in charge, but I am not like that male dog. I will not do what she tells me to do.

I am irritated with the female because she is so close she walks over me. I run through the gate that separates the kitchen from the other floor where the mother's office is. She has now moved my food and water dishes to this room, she has moved the box with the pebbles even further to the basement bathroom where I have privacy. Later, when I return to the main area of the house, the female has changed. She is no longer interested so much in me. She watches, and sometimes follows but now it is at a distance.

The family begins to call me Little Pip. It is now I know with certainty that it is here I am to stay. I sit at the back door often. I hear the mother tell the little girl that they will never let me outside. She talks of coyotes, mountain lions, and the bear that came to the house two weeks ago, dumped the trashcan, and left scat on the front yard. I am sad. I wail at the door. Whenever I do this, the mother picks me up and lessens my distress by kissing my head, stroking my back, holding me close. She tells me she is sorry. I do want to go outside. Yet, I do want to be with this family. I want to stay with the little girl because she is not like the others. There are masses within her, yet there is something more potent that is refining. I think she may have been

The Story of Little Pip

here before, in another time. Her talk is cultivated and stitched with elation. Maybe we shared a life long ago.

It is evening and the family has returned from somewhere. The October sky is dark, but the sharp moon shows me all that I am out of touch with in the backyard. I hear the miniscule living thing under the stove. As the family is coming through the garage door, I coax the mouse out. I hear the family call for me. Usually, when they return from somewhere, I wait at the top of the three stairs behind the gate, but now I stay in the kitchen. They call for me again. I come running to show them I have the teeny one in my mouth. I drop it on the living room carpet and I hear the mom tell the little girl to go upstairs. The little girl sees the mouse, sees that I am picking it up with my mouth, dropping it, batting it with my paws — the little girl shrieks. The mother tells her it's all right and that she will take care of it.

The mouse scampers, I pounce, I put my mouth over it. The mother walks toward me, I drop the mouse, keep it between my paws for her. She takes the teeny one into her hands but I claw at her, I do not want her to take it away. She ignores me, talks in a whisper to her clasped hands. She opens the front door, kneels down, opens her hands and the mouse runs into the darkness. I am angry. The mother tells me she is sorry, I storm away. She is setting the rules, making the marks, and I know she is the lead. I will go to her later, lie and purr on the pillow next to her while she sits on the couch. I will place my paw on top of her arm and in a gentle way, tip my claws into her skin to tell her that I am here, that I know, that I accept.

Rescued Volume 2

I have been here for three months now. The dogs are relaxed, they have never gone after me since that first day. They sleep on their beds in the family room, I sleep on the top of one of the couches. At night, they stay in the mother's room and I walk the house. Sometimes in the morning I stand outside her door and call for her and the little girl. When the father goes into the room to shower, he lets me follow. I leap onto the people bed and snuggle with them as steam fills the open bathroom. I am the third gray one. Three of us, and three of them. Canine, canine, feline. Mother, father, little girl. Only, there are separate forces linking the mother to each one of us.

The mother and me. I curl in her lap when she sits in her office chair and types on her laptop. I purr as she scratches and pets and I bite her hand if she stops. She tells me not to do this but she does not know that I do it because I like her. I want to be on her lap when I see the blinking light on the screen. I want to lie here

The Story of Little Pip

where it is warm. I want to hold onto her because in these moments I have her to myself. Even though she won't let me outside, even though she takes away my teeny ones and releases them, I stay close to her. And I will always stay close to the little girl when she sleeps. She needs the radiance of my body to exceed the illness. While it may not be the reason they brought me to them, I will do this. A better gift, perhaps, than tiny dead creatures. I am now with the mother and little girl, for all time.

The World According to Banzai

I grew up on the mean streets of Citrus Heights, California. They say my mom was a ho cuz none of my five brothers or sisters had the same dad except for me and Eddie. Eddie is an orangie Siamese who looks just like me except his eyes go straight ahead instead of in different directions.

I honed my bug-catching skills on those mean streets, but I was always hungry. Then one night we found a wire box with STINKY GOODNESS inside! It was a trick. The door slammed shut and we could not escape. Some people picked up the wire box with us in it and took us to a jail called "Kill Shelter." It was very loud there with lots of dogs barking, and the wise old geezer tabby next to us said if nobody comes to take you home with them that you get taken through the last door on the right and get sent to the Sausage Factory. He said no cat who

The World According to Banzai

goes through the last door on the right ever comes back. I tried to keep my spirits up, but it's hard when you're worried about becoming bratwurst.

Somewhere along the way I had a really good sleep and when I woke up my boy bits were gone. Eddie's, too. I guess when you're in jail, if you don't guard your boy bits with your life, you lose 'em. The geezer tabby didn't warn us about losing our boy bits cuz he got taken through the last door on the right and we never saw him again. Most of the friends we made in jail got taken through the last door on the right.

Me and Eddie made a pact. We swore that we would practice being adorable and give each other tips on how to improve so that someone would want us and we'd leave through the front door instead of the back. One day, I did. Eddie didn't. I never heard from Eddie or my sisters again. Just in case he went out the last door on the right and got sent to the Sausage Factory, I make a practice of never eating sausage. Or head cheese.

On the day I got my chance to show off my adorableness, the jail people put me in a fun play room and this lady and man came to play with me. I was not that good at playin' yet, cuz when I lived by my wits on the mean streets of Citrus Heights there was not much time for playin'. It was serious work just staying alive. But this playroom was fun with lots of stuff for scratchin' and climbin' and the people were nice and sure enough, they said I was adorable.

But they put me in a jail box and I had to go on a ride in a loud machine. I wasn't really sure what was going on, so all the way for an hour straight I yelled "DON'T

Rescued Volume 2

SEND ME TO THE SAUSAGE FACTORY!!!!" I could tell they were impressed by my vocal prowess and sure enough, we did *not* end up at the Sausage Factory. We ended up at a place that was as big as a fairy tale castle. This place was called "Home." It had good smells, plates piled high with stinky goodness, *heated* cat beds, and my two new brothers, Tripper and Buckaroo.

At Kill Shelter they had named me Danny. The Lady and The Man take the naming ceremony very seriously, and they said that my personality was too big for a lame name like Danny. I required something with a little pizazz.

The first name they thought of was "Reddington" ("Red" for short, cuz I'm kind of a redhead). It is the name of a TV character they like. But The Man decided he didn't want to name me after a murdering sociopath.

Then one day after I was diving off the stairs like a Kamikaze pilot, it hit him. I should be named BANZAI! My brother Buckaroo was originally named Buckaroo Banzai, but then they started calling him Buckaroo

The World According to Banzai

Foobar, and then just Buckaroo. The Banzai name has been hanging out there ever since just waiting for someone to claim it.

Buckaroo is my bestest friend. I was sad when I left my brother Eddie sitting in jail at Kill Shelter, and Buckaroo put his arm around me and explained that Eddie probably went to live with another family instead going to the Sausage Factory. He said that if Eddie was as good as me at being adorable, and as long as he didn't look goofy with eyes that went in different directions like mine, he probably charmed somebody into giving him a nice home. I tried hard to believe that, otherwise I would have been too sad to go on living.

Tripper is a ginormous stripey cat who was born in the forest and decided that The Man and lady needed to make him their cat. I think tuna was involved. They say he was really wild when he was a kitten and it took The Lady months to lure him with stinky goodness to get close enough so she could touch him. The first time he was inside the house he climbed inside the grand piano to get away from the sister-in-law's screechy laughing. Tripper sez her laughing would make anyone do crazy things like climb inside the piano.

Once The Lady got Tripper to trust her, they took him to the stabby place and stole Tripper's boy bits. He was mad about that, and when he got home he ran away to live back in the forest for a couple of days, but then he got hungry and decided he wanted Fancy Feast more than he wanted to stay mad at The Man and The Lady. Tripper sez that life is full of choices and you have to keep the End Game in mind. You can tell Tripper

Rescued Volume 2

is smart cuz he is always saying philosophical stuff like that.

He's also ginormous. He weighs 22 pounds. I can only dream of getting a physique like that. Boy, if I weighed 22 pounds I would be the envy of every mancat I know. Unfortunately, I am not very big-boned. Tripper has what they call a "generous build."

Whenever I see Tripper, I run up to him and bow my head down so he can lick it, and then I put my butt in his face so he can sniff it. It is our ritual. Tripper sez that it should be a reciprocal arrangement. Unfortunately, his butt is gross. He's too ginormous to groom it properly, so there are always some Klingons back there. The Lady has to squint her face into a million wrinkles and use the flea comb to tidy him up. Sometimes she gets the clippers and gives him a boyzillian. Tripper sez there's nothing better than a little manscaping, and he claims that it makes his boy bits look bigger.

This is not true. He is too tubby to actually *see* his nether regions, much less groom them, and he does not seem to remember that he said adios to his boy bits long ago. I am not gonna be the one to remind him of that.

As a tribute to the great neurosurgeon-physicist-action hero Buckaroo Banzai, me and Buckaroo run the Banzai Institute. At the Banzai Institute we strive to keep the world free of Red Lectroids. I spend much of my day on the grounds of the Banzai Institute sharpening my skills in finding Red Lectroids by hunting for bugs and lizzerds. I do not understand why Fancy Feast does not have a lizzerd flavor cuz lizzerds are delicious.

The World According to Banzai

Okay, I'll admit they are a little dry and stringy, but if you like jerky, you will love lizzerds.

The hunt for Red Lectroids is fraught with peril. I have never seen one in my whole entire life, but Tripper sez they are even fiercer than those vishus deer. Tripper sez vishus deer eat tender yung joosy cats, and if they catch me they will eat all of me except for my tail. Tripper sez vishus deer scrape all the fur and meat off of cats' tails and then make necklaces out of the bones. It is a good thing I have never seen a vishus deer, cuz if I did I might wet my pants. If I wore pants.

That great Feline Life Coach Max Thompson (author of several books including *The Rules: A Guide for People Owned by Cats*) sez that real live fresh dead Red Lectroids taste like chicken but afterward you'll spend hours picking the scales from your teeth. And you'll have Red Lectroid breath for *days*. And flatulence. I don't know what flatulence is, but the way Max says it, I don't want to find out.

As you can plainly see, it is very good that I have wizened old cats around to mentor me about stuff like flatulence and vishus deer.

To acquire some life skills and learn to *eat* dinner, not *be* dinner, I joined Cat Scouts. It's an online community where cats learn valuable scouting skills, earn badges and socialize with other Cat Scouts. Cat Scouts is very challenging. If you are a hooligan, you get demerits and risk getting kicked out. Buckaroo got about a million demerits once when he made The Man climb into a bunch of poison oak to rescue him in the forest.

Rescued Volume 2

The siren call of shenanigans is always ringing in my ears so it is a challenge for me to be a good Cat Scout. Once I got eleventy demerits for something I didn't even do.

See, every night these friendly tuxie cat creatures with ginormous floofy tails and impressive white racing stripes down their backs come to hang out on the back deck of The Institute. The Lady calls them The Skunks. I guess that is their family name. None of them seems to have a first name. The Lady goes out and sits down with a glass of wine every night and talks to them. She is a Skunk whisperer.

Of course I wanted to go up and do the mutual butt sniffing thing to get to know them better. One night it didn't go so good. I guess Skunk ate something that didn't agree with him and when I sniffed his butt he farted and squirted fart juice in my face. A few minutes later The Man came and got me cuz he thought I needed rescuing, which clearly I did not because I am a big mancat who relishes stuff like farts and burps. But

The World According to Banzai

he grabbed me and the worst night of my whole entire life commenced. He gave me a bath.

Humans seem to love their baths. If you watch the TV, you might have seen that thing where a man called ED takes a little blue pill and then he and his lady are in bathtubs on a hilltop watching the sunset and tinkly music plays. You have to take a little blue pill to get brave enough to go into a bathtub full of water.

My bath was not on a hilltop and there was no tinkly music or blue pill. It was in the kitchen sink where Tripper and Buckaroo could have seen me if they didn't mind smelling the fart juice. The Lady asked The Google how to get fart juice out of cat furs, and The Google told her the recipe for a magic potion that made the stink go away. Sure enough, the stink circled down the drain with my dignity.

I spent the next few days trying to lick away the wets and get myself dry. Well, I guess really it was just a couple of hours, but it seemed like days.

I hate the wets. I will never earn a Swimming Merit Badge in Cat Scouts. But I have earned badges in Boxing, Tree Climbing, Power Napping, Gardening, Wildlife Observation and Insect Study.

Buckaroo is kind of a legend in Cat Scouts, cuz he was the first scout to earn the Swimming Merit Badge. He is a good swimmer. He can swim all the way across the cement pond in our backyard.

On the grounds of the Banzai Institute there is a good climbing tree. It is funny to climb up to where the branches won't hardly hold me any longer and then watch The Lady acting all scared and worried that I'm gonna fall. That always means that she'll go back in the house and then come out with some good treats to lure me down. Not cheapo grocery store treats, but the freeze-dried real meat ones that we don't get very often cuz they're expensive.

People are not smart enough to realize when you are training them to do your bidding. I have trained the The Lady to bring me treats after I climb up into the tiny branches part of the tree. The higher I climb, the more treats I get. If I cry like a girlcat, I get even more treats. Tripper sez it's okay to cry like a girlcat if there are treats involved.

The Man must be even less smart because I have not been successful in training him to bring me treats when I get high in the tree. He just looks up, says, "Hey Banzai whatcha doin' up there?" and goes back to doing his piddling around in the backyard which is where he hangs out on the weekends so The Lady won't make him do chores.

One thing that concerns me is that at night when I get locked up inside the house, there is no one outside to patrol the grounds of the Banzai Institute. I yell at the top of my lungs to express how imperative it is that I go outside to patrol, but the people tell me to shut up. And that's when they're being polite. Sometimes they say it with words from the Bad Words List.

Because security on the grounds of The Institute is nonexistent at night, many intruders sneak up and eat the dog food on the deck. That is just a ruse they use so they can hang out and peer inside and steal trade secrets from The Institute. You can tell they are up to NO GOOD cuz they wear masks over their beady eyes.

The people are not very bright about the intruders. They put out dog food for them like a big ole welcome mat. But the intruders hang around even after the dog food is gone and look inside the windows with sad and hungry faces like one of those Big Eyes paintings. The people cannot say No to those sad Big Eyes faces, so they give them some more dog food.

I think the intruders are trying to steal our Wi-Fi. I yell out the window at them, "IF YOU WANT FREE WI-FI, GO TO STARBUCKS," but the louder I yell, the more The Lady yells at me not to yell. What the heck is an "inside voice," anyway, and why would I want to use one? The intruders are OUTSIDE. Clearly, they will not hear me unless I use an *outside* voice.

Buckaroo helps me with my job as Chief Patrol Cat, but his main job is "Cat Loc8tor Tester." We each have transponders on our collars so that if we get kidnapped by Red Lectroids, we can be tracked to the alien planet where we are being held hostage. Buckaroo's job is to sneak away to a neighbor's yard, then wait until The Man hunts him down using the tricorder that communicates with the transponder and identifies Buckaroo's location.

But mostly, Buckaroo just hangs out on the deck of the Zalmeski's house where they give him treats. Sometimes he makes it *really* interesting by taking his collar off and leaving it under the Zalmeski's deck while he goes to hang out in the big-ass bass boat that's parked in the driveway next door. Boy, is The Man ever surprised when the tricorder homes in on the little red beacon only to find that there's no Buckaroo attached to it! We always get a big laff outta that.

I confess, it can be challenging living with an inferior species. We haven't yet perfected translator technology and it's not uncommon for communication to break down.

Like the other day, Tripper had a mousie as an appetizer before dinner. He was kind enough to leave the gutz for me on the doormat. He said, "C'mon over here, pipsqueak, and take a whiff of this!"

I have never smelt anything so wonderful in my whole entire life. Those gutz smelt SO great that I rolled in them so I could take the smell with me wherever I went. I rolled on the new white carpet by my scratching post to get the smell there, too. And then on the fuzzy blanket on the TV couch. And then I rubbed against The Lady.

In retrospect, rubbing against The Lady was a mistake. I underestimated how loud she could scream. The problem is, I don't understand *why* she screamed. Here are the possibilities:

1. She was PO'd cuz I didn't save the gutz in a ziplock bag for her so she could put them in the big cold food box in the kitchen and let them get good and ripe in the crisper drawer until six months later they turn to soup and she has to throw them out.

2. They were too fresh (and therefore, insufficiently aromatic) when I brought them into the house on my furs cuz everyone knows they're better when they've been left marinating in the sun for a few days.

The World According to Banzai

3. She was really excited cuz I'd finally caught my first mouse (not that I would ever take credit for one of Tripper's conquests).

The bottom line is, you can be the most brilliant astrophysicist neurosurgeon in the universe and not understand wimmin.

And then there's her singing.

She puts these white strings in her ears when she does stuff around the house, and the minute those strings go in, you know your eardrums are about to be assaulted by sounds that are worse than an Accordion Bagpipe Band. It is called "singing."

The first time I heard her singing I thought it was a 911 emergency cuz it sounded like that time The Man was watching that *Texas Chainsaw Massacre* movie on TV. The Man came down the stairs and asked her if she was okay, and she said she was just singing. I guess he had never heard singing before cuz he said, "Is that what you call it?"

She just put the white strings back in her ears and cranked up the volume.

I was surprised to discover that her singing sounded strangely like the sounds made by those stripey fart juice creatures outside when they go on piggyback rides with each other. Buckaroo sez it's more like fingernails on a blackboard. Tripper doesn't weigh in on that; he just hides in the closet under the beach towels.

Sometimes when the dark part of the day comes, The Lady and The Man watch TV. The TV is a magical box where miniature people — people even smaller than cats — live. When The Man watches it there are explosions and gunfire but we are safe because we are not inside the TV box.

I always watch the TV with them. I sleep on the fuzzy blanket I got mouse gutz on (even though The Lady put it in the washer machine and made the mouse gutz go away so it isn't aromatic anymore), and every once in a while I climb on The Man and purr, which he seems to like. Buckaroo sez it's good to climb on the people a couple of times a day and purr and make biscuits and lick them on the mouth. Well, I'm not a baby anymore, so I won't make biscuits like Buckaroo does, and I won't lick them on the mouth cuz I don't want to get people spit on me. But I am a purring machine!

Not to toot my own horn, but I am also excellent at the fine art of shedding. Shedding is when you put your excess furs on furniture. That's how FURniture got its name. And it's really easy! I just jump on the blue couch in the fireplace room and my furs come off on it and pretty soon it is almost white with furs and very soft. The Lady encourages me by using the cat toy sucker-upper machine to get all the furs off so I can do it again and hone my shedding skills.

Sometimes she finds a whisker and she saves it cuz she sez it's good luck. I don't like losing whiskers, though, cuz I am not really blessed in the facial hair department like Tripper is. He has a real mancat set of whiskers. Kinda like that Sam Elliott guy's moustache. Tripp sez I just need to give it time and once I am through being a teenager I will have my own mancat set of whiskers.

The World According to Banzai

Buckaroo is almost three years old, so he has a lot of wisdom and stories stored up inside him. He says it is his responsibility to keep stories alive about The Cats Who Came Before, and hand down these stories to the younger generation. That would be me.

One of The Cats Who Came Before was Skeezix, a famous big-eared Oriental cat who lived with The Man and The Lady many years before I was borned. He was one of the first cat bloggers and he was responsible for getting hundreds of cats around the world into blogging. Blogging and Instagram are very important steps toward Kitteh World Domination.

Buckaroo knew Skeezix for about two weeks before Skeezix went to The Bridge because of tummy toomers. Buckaroo was in a box of kittens being given away, and The Lady rescued him. She picked him cuz he had a couple of mocha patches on his white fur, just like Skeezix. At that time, they were in the process of saying good-bye to Skeezix and she knew that a big gaping hole in her heart would need to be filled. It was that moment when she realized that was why Buckaroo was sent to her. That is called fate and karma. Fate is when things happen for a reason. Karma is when you throw good stuff (or bad stuff) out into the universe, and get good stuff (or bad stuff) in return.

When Skeezix was gone, Buckaroo knew he needed to step up and fill the hole that was left in the hearts of The Man and The Lady. They were both very sad; their faces were wet every day, especially The Man's. Skeezix was his best buddy and they were always together. They would have been Siamese twins if The Man had been a Siamese cat. Buckaroo sure had his work cut out for him.

Even though he was just a kitten, Buckaroo knew what to do. Cats are smart that way. First, he put The Man on a strict regimen of playtime. He worked him out until The Man lost all feeling in his arms from swinging the fishing pole bird toy. Second, every single morning he climbed onto the people bed and gave The Lady a kiss on the mouth to say "Good Morning." (Buckaroo does not have the same aversion to people spit that I do.) Third, he devised a schedule chock full of purr therapy. Every time he saw one of them sit down, he'd be there, motor running.

It worked. At first he wasn't sure, cuz they still had their sad faces on a lot of the time. But he stuck with it and they began to smile more and he made them laugh. Because of Buckaroo's excellent tutelage, I was well prepared when it was my turn to fill the holes left in their hearts. This time their 18-year-old geezer meezer cat, Mao, went to The Bridge.

The first thing I did was make cute, cross-eyed faces at the people. Since my eyes go in different directions, Buckaroo sez I should use that fault to my advantage and milk it for all it's worth becuz it amuses people when they see cats with funny eyes like mine. So whenever The Man or The Lady is around, I look at my nose with both eyes at the same time like I'm concentrating on a fly at the tip of it. Every single time they see me doing that, they smile and say something like, "You are such a cutie!"

The second thing I did was start panting after I play hard. Panting is easy to do. You just stick out your

The World According to Banzai

tongue and breathe real fast. Whenever I do that, The Man calls out to The Lady and says, "Honey, you've got to see this!" Then they both stare at me with smiles on their faces while I pant and sometimes The Lady runs and gets her camera because she sez it is a "Kodak moment."

The third thing is definitely NOT on Buckaroo's Mend-a-Broken-Heart plan. But I have good instincts and sensed it would work: I let them rub my tummy. When I'm curled up in my cat bed and they come over, I roll over a bit to invite them to snorgle my belly. When they do, I purr and lick their hands and stretch out until I'm twice as long as normal and then fall asleep on my back, which is one of the Official Cute Cat Positions according to the Cats of Instagram (aka #catsofinstagram). The people smile really big when I do that and The Lady calls me her little creamsicle. Whenever I see my adorableness reflected in their eyes, I know that the hole in their hearts is getting smaller and smaller.

So The Man and The Lady rescued me from The Sausage Factory and I rescued them from The Sads. I helped them focus on moving forward rather than dwelling on something they had no control over. I got the best home in the world out of the deal, and even better, a real family.

Some days, when I'm all alone and thinking Deep Thoughts, I wonder about Eddie. I hope he got a chance to rescue someone. Maybe one day I'll see him on #catsofinstagram and know for sure.

Pounce Takes a Chance

When it comes to humans, you never know for sure. A cat on the street meets a lot of different people, and you need to learn what you're dealing with. But in the end, you have to make your best choice and then have faith, because the alternative is to stay out here, in the urban wasteland. It's wild and unpredictable, and I didn't like it.

I wanted to go home, but I didn't know where home was. I was all turned around and although I combed and searched through hundreds of city blocks, I felt like I kept ending up in the same place: somewhere that's vaguely familiar, but still not home. People will tell you that cats have some kind of homing device and can find their way around really well using their keen sense of smell. Nope. That's dogs. Seriously, though, this whole "cats can take care of themselves" shtick is so old. We sold ourselves so well as pets, into the homes and hearts of people everywhere, that we're sometimes invisible. We're victims of our own PR.

Realizing finally that I was lost, I decided to look around for someone to rescue me. I spent nights sleeping in a cemetery and days scanning the local streets and businesses for anyone that I thought might help me out. There wasn't much. A couple of restaurants (where cats are never welcome), some wholesale storefronts, a resale store. And then there was a small body shop where the workers all seemed to come from some far off land. They were always busy and although they were kind of loud and gruff, they looked like they enjoyed working together and besides, like I said, there weren't that many choices.

So I wandered into the body shop, announcing myself as I always did whenever I arrived anywhere. After all, how would anyone notice me, absorbed as they were in their business, if I didn't announce myself?

At the sound of my voice, work came to a halt. The crash of banging metal, the high-pitched hum of drills, the clang of wrenches — all slowly ceased. And I realized that everyone's eyes were resting on me.

"It's a cat," said one of the men, peering out over the hood of a car.

"A black cat" said another with a paint sprayer in his hand. "Bad luck."

"That is a superstition," said a deeper voice from behind me. I turned and looked up, and up, and up still further, at a very large man with a thick accent

Pounce Takes a Chance

who gazed down at me. "This little guy needs help. He is hungry. And lost."

"What should we feed him?" asked one of the guys.

"Where can he stay? A body shop is no place for a cat."

The big man looked down at me with concern, and maybe a hint of a smile. Slowly, he leaned down toward me, extending his hand. I eagerly moved toward him and gently nuzzled the top of my head against his palm. Satisfied at my friendly display, the man stood back up to his full height.

"There is that lady who lives down the street, the one who brought her car in after she got into an accident. She volunteers at a shelter and helps cats on the street. She will know what to do. I'll go see if she is home." He turned and left.

I remained where I was. Things appeared to be progressing splendidly. My chosen humans had shown no signs of wanting to harm me, nor had they shooed me away. The large man who had gone to fetch the cat lady seemed helpful, and the others, while somewhat bewildered by my sudden appearance, were also friendly and benevolent chaps. One of them ran a few doors down to a small corner grocery and brought me a can of tuna. I can't say that I'm really partial to tuna, but I was very hungry, and I quickly devoured some of it while most of the men got back to what they were doing before I had arrived on the scene.

There it was: that feeling of discomfort in my stomach, as though something already occupied the space where the food was supposed to go. I had been experiencing this sensation whenever I found something to eat for the past couple of days. I suspected it might have something to do with some stuff I ate a few nights before, when I was feeling especially down and out and there was nothing at all I could find to satisfy my hunger — two small pieces of wood, and a length of some kind of wire that had a colored covering. I knew that these were not food, but I so wanted the feeling of eating something, of having something other than air in my belly that I swallowed them anyway. Since then, I had developed the sense that something wasn't quite right in there. But I didn't throw up the food I ate and I didn't really feel sick, so I ignored it.

There was a puddle of sunlight on the concrete floor of the shop a few feet back from the sliding door on the front of the garage. I moved into the light, circled, and then lay down on the warm concrete. It felt good. I remembered the safety of home, the comforting warmth in the winter and the cool shade in the summer. I remembered food bowls that were never empty and secure places to nap. All gone. Somehow I had managed to pass through some kind of portal, where my former life had disappeared into the rainy sheen and foggy breath of a city at night.

It made me sad, so I stopped thinking those thoughts right away. It would do me no good to look back. Besides, things had not gone all that badly for me up to this point. It's true that I'd lost quite a bit of weight and that I was tired, but I already had made it for several months out in the world. Some of the friends I'd met along the way hadn't.

Pounce Takes a Chance

The sun tracing my back and my head and my tail and my outstretched front paws brought me back to the present. It whispered, *You are all right. Right now, this very minute, you are perfectly all right.* The thought calmed me. I closed my eyes as I recited this little mantra, until it dissolved into a low, soft purr.

I don't know how much time went by; I must have drifted into a gentle sleep, because next thing I knew, there was some kind of hubbub in the garage. I opened my eyes to see the large, helpful mechanic looking at me. Standing next to him was a woman. She had brown hair pulled back into a ponytail and a sharp face. But her eyes were kind and they made me feel safe. In her hand was something that I recognized: a cat carrier.

"He's a beautiful cat, Muhammed" she said. "The shelter will take him in tomorrow morning. We can't bring him now, so he'll have to stay here, overnight, in this carrier."

So there it was. I'd spend the night in the carrier. Not something I looked forward to, but if you want to come in from the cold, if you want a shot at the food bowls and blankets and someone to cuddle with at night, you have to do some stuff, maybe, that you don't want to do. As a free cat, I had a choice: I could have walked out of the garage and wandered off down the street, but I wasn't going to give up the chance at getting a home again. Not this cat. So I let the nice woman place me in the carrier and I settled in for the duration. It was quiet in the garage at night, but I could still hear the sounds of city busses and other traffic going by. Sitting in the carrier, I thought about how amazing this world can sometimes be. You get outside, you get lost. You find a human or humans you think can help you and you take a chance. And if you're lucky, you get help.

It was cramped in the carrier. The lady had put in the plate with the tuna for me, and not only did I spill the tuna juice, I got it all over my coat. And I felt the uncomfortable sensations in my belly. *Why had I eaten those things?* I thought to myself. *And how to get help with it?* I sensed that things might not be okay if I didn't manage to let someone know there was a problem soon. But I am by nature an optimistic cat, and so far things had gone well. I had to believe that I would be all right, and once I got to the shelter, I would be helped. I sat, listening to the sounds of the city night, my eyes half-closed, and purred to comfort myself. After awhile I drifted off to sleep. In no time, strips of sunlight began to filter through the glass bricks on the side of the garage. It was almost time for the next phase of my journey.

The lady arrived early in the morning in her car, the car that Muhammad had recently repaired. They loaded my carrier onto the back seat, and the three of us took the short drive over to the shelter.

I was feeling optimistic, but a little nervous. I would have preferred to meet my new caregivers in a little better condition. I am no matinee idol, but I consider myself a fairly handsome cat, and it was embarrassing to meet new people in this state: thin, bedraggled, and covered in tuna juice. To combat my anxiety, I began

Pounce Takes a Chance

to talk loudly on the trip to the shelter. Muhammed looked back at me.

"It is okay, little man" he said. "You are going to be okay."

When we arrived at the shelter, a worker answered the door and invited us all inside. Immediately I was overwhelmed by the scent of a hundred cats, and that's not an exaggeration. Peering out from the door of my carrier I saw that there were cats lounging around the reception area, some sitting on chairs, some perched in cat trees. I relaxed a little as I realized that these cats were not confined to cages. I figured that I would be in a cage for a while, but it was comforting to know that once I was resident here, I'd be able to roam freely and do my own thing.

While paperwork was being filled out the worker took my carrier back to another room, where I would be checked into the clinic. He placed my carrier on a table and opened the door.

"Come on out, little guy" he said. He seemed nice, so I slowly emerged from the carrier in my less than pristine state. The guy looked me over. He petted me and ran his hands over me and around by body.

"You're a bit thin," he said softly. Then he noticed how wet I was and smelled his hand.

"You're going to need a bath," he said. "Let's do that before we get you checked in."

He took me to another sink with a grill, over it and proceeded to wet me down, soap me up, and rinse me off. I was really happy to get the tuna juice off of me, and I started up with my singing again.

"You have a lot to say, don't you?" said the shelter worker. I responded with a happy vocal salute.

"I have to give you a name," he said, looking me over after toweling my fur to sop up the excess water. It felt so good to be clean, and somewhere that I was safe. I just kept chirping along while he watched me, thinking out loud.

"You're kind of thin now and a little disheveled, but you seem like a happy cat. I want to give you a name that will fit you when you're feeling better. That will reflect who you are." We stood looking at each other for a few minutes; he lost in thought and me chirping loudly. I've always thought that when you put your best foot forward with a sunny disposition, that people will respond well. Suddenly, a smile came over his face.

"You're telling me your name, aren't you? I'm going to name you Pounce."

"Pounce! Pounce!" I said eagerly. It sounded like a good name, and I was happy with it.

After that I went through the check-in process. I was weighed, my temperature was taken, I was examined for wounds, received flea treatment, tested for FIV/FeLV, scanned for a microchip, and other routine things. All the while I kept merrily singing out my new name. It felt good to have an identity again. When you're a random cat on the street, you become invisible. No one knows who you are and although you are no less real, you fade into an anonymous background as far as the day-to-day human world is concerned. Getting a new name was the first step of my reentry into that

Pounce Takes a Chance

world, back to a place where someone cares about you. Back home.

After my checkup, I was placed in a cage in an intake unit with other cats that had recently been admitted to the shelter. We were observed to make sure we didn't have any contagious illness, and I remained in my cage until it was time for my second round of vaccines. The set up was good — there was enough room for my litter box and food, as well as space for me get up and walk around a bit. After the confines of the carrier it seemed huge.

Once at the shelter my life quickly settled into a routine. I was fed three times daily. In the mornings, people emptied my litter box, cleaned out my cage, and gave me a fresh towel. Clinic workers came in once a day to make sure I was eating, give me some attention, and generally see if I was doing well. Life seemed to be pretty good.

By the third day something weird began to happen: the fur around the edges of my ears began peeling back, leaving exposed skin. It was pronounced enough that the shelter manager was brought in to take a look. She stood, examining me for a while. "He's eating well, using his litter box, and seems to be in good spirits."

"POUNCE!" I exclaimed, right on cue.

"Hopefully it's not ringworm "she said. The room came to a momentary standstill. Ringworm is something that cats can get while they're on the street, and it's not welcome anywhere — not because it's that serious, but because it's infectious and takes a long time to treat. I'd heard that cats had even been put down at shelters because they had ringworm. But this was not that kind of shelter. At least that's what I heard from Horace, the gregarious and debonair tuxedo cat in the cage across from me. But I didn't want to be treated and isolated and besides, I knew that wasn't what was going on. I knew it had something to do with what I had eaten. But how to let these nice people know that?

I told Horace about my problem. He listened carefully, sitting back on his haunches. "That is a problem" he said. "But you don't feel ill?"

I shook my head. "But I'm losing fur on my ears. I feel it in my stomach sometimes, when I eat. But I don't throw up and the food seems to pass through okay."

"Well, don't worry," he said. "You'll see Dr. Castillo."

"Dr. Castillo? Who is that?"

"He's the veterinarian who comes in on Friday and checks everyone out. The newer cats all get seen by him before they move up to the adoption floor. I'm sure he'll be able to figure it out."

So maybe things would be okay after all. The truth was, I was beginning to feel a little less good. Now that I had time to relax and not look over my shoulder all the time, like you have to out on the street, I realized that my back legs were a little weak and a little messed up. They didn't work quite the way I wanted them to. My hips were a little rubbery. It was hard to understand what that had to do with what I had swallowed. The same with my ears. What could be happening to me?

I lay in my cage and tried to console myself by purring. There was nothing I could do to change things right

Pounce Takes a Chance

then. Everything had gone my way since I'd decided to chance getting help from the humans. Surely this would work out as well.

On Friday morning, a rush of excitement spread through the intake ward. Everyone was up a little earlier than usual, eating their breakfast and using their litter boxes, then primping and grooming as they waited to see Dr. Castillo. For many of us, it was our first time seeing him. Some wouldn't need another exam. Others, like Horace, who had arrived with a bit of a skin condition, were getting rechecked to see how the prescribed medications were helping.

I was nervous. I needed Dr. Castillo to find out about the wire I had eaten. I didn't know what would happen next, but I knew that if I could let the vet know what was happening, there was a chance he could help me. The fur on my ears was actually a little better. Not totally, but it hadn't gotten worse and everyone was pretty much convinced that I did not have ringworm.

My thoughts were interrupted by the sudden arrival of the same clinic worker who had checked me in and named me when I had arrived at the shelter.

"Hello, Pounce. Time for your exam!" he said.

"Pounce!" I nervously responded. But I was happy to see him. I liked him and he seemed to like me. During the week he'd come to the intake room a few times to visit me and pet me. Now he placed me in a carrier and took me back to the shelter clinic to see the doctor.

Rescued Volume 2

Dr. Castillo was not that old, with curly hair and a mustache, and a friendly face. He was a jovial man that was quick to laugh.

"Who is this guy?" he asked.

"Pounce! Pounce!" I yelled, wanting to get off on the right foot. Dr. Castillo scratched the top of my head with his fingers and gazed down at me with a twinkle in his eye.

"His name is Pounce," said the shelter guy. He held me for my exam while the doctor looked at my eyes and ears. He noted the missing fur on my ears, but didn't say anything about it. He listened to my heart and lungs with a stethoscope, and so far it seemed like everything was okay. Then came the part of the exam where he felt around my abdomen. Because I was still underweight he could easily feel my stomach, kidneys, and other stuff inside of me.

"Whoa," said the doctor suddenly. He closed his eyes and I felt him kind of digging his fingers in on either side of the area below my ribcage.

"This cat needs an x-ray," he said. "There's definitely something in there that shouldn't be." A wave of relief came over me as I heard his words. I was put back into the carrier and taken to the x-ray machine in the basement.

The x-rays showed everything I had consumed: the pieces of wire, the little chunks of wood, all eaten when I was desperate and scared and had no real prospect of being rescued.

"That needs to come out of there right away," said Dr. Castillo. "It's just sitting in his stomach. The wire

Pounce Takes a Chance

might have some kind of protective coating on it, but his stomach acid is breaking it down and the wire may be poisoning him. That's the reason for the fur loss and the weakness in his back legs. I need to take him back to my practice this afternoon. We'll put him under anesthesia and I'll try to fish that stuff out with a scope. Since it's still in his stomach, we might not have to cut him open to get it."

"Do you think he'll be okay?" asked the shelter worker who had named me. I looked up at him and saw that his face was full of concern. It was then that I realized that he had been watching me carefully this whole time, monitoring my progress. I wondered if maybe, just maybe...but no, I couldn't think of anything like that right now. I had surgery to get through.

An IV line was placed in my leg, and I was given fluids so that I would ready for the surgery later that afternoon. When it was time for the doctor to leave, I was put back into a carrier with my fluids in tow. As we drove away, I watched as the clinic people I'd come to know over the past week waved at me. I was glad they had found out what was wrong with me. I knew it had to be fixed, but I hadn't planned on anything like this.

I don't remember a lot after that. It all happened very quickly. One minute I was being taken from the carrier and my IV reattached, and the next I was groggy and struggling to wake up. Slowly it dawned on me that the whole thing was over; I was waking up and it was done.

"Hey there," said Dr. Castillo as he saw me moving around. "You're going to be okay, fella." On the table next to him were the contents of my stomach: two pieces of wire with the covering wearing away. One was silver, the other copper colored. And next to it were the small chunks of wood. I could hardly believe that it was all real. Slowly I curled up and let myself drift back to sleep.

🐾 🐾 🐾

Back at the shelter I was some kind of rock star. The shelter workers moved me to a cage in the clinic for my recovery, and I only had to spend a few days there before I was given the okay for the adoption floor. All the workers brought me extra food and spent more time playing with me. The other cats gathered around to hear the story of my life on the street and my surgery with Dr. Castillo. Some of them I recognized from my time in the intake ward. Horace was there, and he congratulated me heartily, like a long lost friend.

"Now all we need to do is find a home, old man," he said as he gave me a welcome back headbutt. I realized he was right. Since I had first seen the auto body shop and decided to take a chance on some friendly people, I had known that my final destination would be a new home, a safe place with lots of blankets and plenty of food. But now that it was time, I was worried that might not happen very soon. The fact is, people don't look at black cats the way they do at the playful tabbies and fiery calicos. Some still think we're bad luck. Even those who know better somehow don't see us the same way they see other cats. Even with good manners and a stellar personality, black cats often just sit at shelters, waiting and waiting to be adopted.

Pounce Takes a Chance

But something else was bothering me too. Since I had taken a chance on people, I had seen nothing but their good side. Muhammed, the friendly cat lady, and everyone at that shelter had helped me so much. And I didn't want to go back out and risk ending up on the street again. I wanted to stay here with these nice people, like the worker who had named me, and my new pals, like Horace. Would I find someone to adopt me who was just as nice, or would I wind up lost and desperate like before?

One day after I'd been back at the shelter for a week or so, my worker friend came and picked me up. He looked into my eyes as he held me.

"You did so good, Pounce," he said. "You really lived up to your name. Such a great, happy cat. You know, it's time for you to go home. " I could see that his eyes were a little watery as he spoke. "You need a good home, where you'll be loved and cherished forever. You can't stay here, even though it is a nice place."

I looked up at him and realized that he had never once stopped following my progress since that day he'd checked me in and named me. Maybe the hunch I'd had before my surgery was right.

"Would you like to come live with me?" he asked. I thought I hadn't heard him right. Could he really be saying that he'd take me home? Could it really be?

"Pounce! Pounce!" I nuzzled my nose against his neck.

🐾 🐾 🐾

Like I said, when it comes to humans, you never really know for sure. I took my chances and they all worked out well. I know how lucky I am. Sitting here in the window of the apartment that is now home, I watch the play lot next door, searching for squirrels that run across the ground and up into the trees that line the block. Those same trees drop their leaves in the autumn, driving me crazy. I run back and forth across the windowsill yelling at the leaves as they corkscrew their way from branch to earth.

My human still works with animals. Every few years I get a new brother or sister that he has helped nurse back to health and then just can't say goodbye to. My friend Horace ended up here as well, and now we are more than friends, we are brothers.

Once in a while, at night, I lie on the couch and listen to the sounds out in the street just as I did that night in the carrier at the auto body shop. Only now, I don't have to wonder where I'm headed or what my life will be like. I think about the other cats out there, lost and scared, and I close my eyes and make a secret wish for them to find peace and love, safety and security, just like I did. And then I lay my head down, snuggle into the couch cushion, and let sleep come over me like a warm, soft blanket.

Ashton: A Scary Situation

Humans are scary.

My mother taught me that. She took good care of me and my brother as little kittens. Being with her made me feel safe and warm from the inside. And she taught us that humans are scary.

As we grew, our mother was away more often, hunting food for us. My brother and I would spend the time napping under the thick shrubbery that we called home or playing in the surrounding tall grass. My brother would pounce so hard that he'd knock me flat against the soil and I would smell like growing things and sunshine. Even though I am a brown tabby with wide, black stripes that hid the dirt, I would bathe and bathe until I smelled right again. Until I smelled like me, my brother, and my mother again.

Rescued Volume 2

One day, while stalking my brother in the tall grass, I heard a noise. Big, crunching footsteps approached, so loud that I knew whatever made them was far too large to be a cat, a squirrel, or even a raccoon.

Crunch. I froze in place, listening. *Crunch.* I flattened myself against the ground even though it was going to make me smell like soil and I would need another bath. *Crunch.* Now I could see it approaching, huge and towering: a human.

Humans are scary.

I was suddenly very glad that humans were also loud, so that I knew when one came near me.

The human had no fur on its arms or around its eyes. Didn't it get cold without fur? As I watched, it made deep, booming mouth sounds. I watched, hoping it would keep crunching past me, but it stopped. The human stood between me and the shrubbery that my mother, my brother and I called home. Even worse, the human's eyes were looking right at me!

Humans are scary.

The human lurched toward me, making mouth sounds again, and so much fear filled me that it didn't all fit inside my little body, making my fur stand on end. My tail puffed out thickly with black and brown rings like a raccoon's. I dug my little claws into the soil and spun around before running in the opposite direction, away from my home.

Crunch. Crunch. It was right behind me!

I ran as fast as my little striped legs could carry me. The tall grass slashed against my nose and whiskers, but I kept going as the long-legged thing chased behind

Ashton: A Scary Situation

me. I could still hear the booming mouth sounds even though my ears were pinned back in flight.

I was running full speed away from the horrible mouth sounds when the ground beneath my paws changed from soil to something hard and cold to the touch. The noises changed too, filling my ears with a fearsome rumbling noise. Huge things on wheels roared past faster than I could possibly run.

I skidded to a stop, heart thumping, and turned to look behind me. The human was still there, its mouth sounds barely audible over the roar at my back. It slowed and crouched as it approached, then bent down, big paws reaching for me.

Humans are scary!

With a squeaking meow that vanished under the rumbling noise, I spun and darted in among the huge things that followed the hard surface. As I fled, I spotted something dark, like a hole, on the far side of the hard ground. A kitten could take shelter in a hole like that! I hurried toward it.

My tiny paws raced as fast as they could across the hard surface, and I was nearly to the dark hole when I heard a loud squeal and felt blinding pain.

I lay on my side, panting, hurting everywhere. My head felt so heavy I could hardly lift it, and when I did, pain banged harder along the left side of my face. I couldn't see at all from my left eye. Alarmed, I tried to stand, but my limp rear legs wouldn't obey.

I pushed myself up on my front paws, trying to focus. The big things kept rumbling past. A gust from an especially large one blew me over sideways.

Rescued Volume 2

The hole I had been trying to reach looked invitingly close, and I tried to crawl with only my front legs, my little claws sliding across the pebbles embedded in the rough surface.

A movement off to my right caught my attention and I turned my head to look. My only working eye wouldn't focus completely, but the tallness and lumbering gait of the moving thing told me another human was approaching behind me.

Humans are scary.

I scrambled harder toward the dark hole, splintering my claws as I dragged myself a cat's length closer. But my back legs wouldn't push me, and my progress was too slow. The human could move faster than I could!

The constant howl of the huge things rushing nearby masked the sound of any footfalls, so I didn't know the human had reached for me until I felt its big paws surround and lift me.

I could hear mouth sounds from the human over the rumbling noise, sounding something like "Dontbitemedontbitemedontbiteme" as I thrashed, terrified, in its paws. It placed me into a container with low sides.

I meowed with alarm as the entire container lurched up off of the ground and the human's mouth sounds continued. This human sounded different than the other one, and I wondered how many were going to chase me today. The human lowered me, container and all, into one of those huge things on wheels, and after a final slamming noise, it was quieter, the rumbling sounds becoming softer and muffled.

Ashton: A Scary Situation

I raised my painful head as the scary human sat down next to me. The human had bare arms and paws, and a bare face too, underneath the dark fur on top of its head. Its round eyes, the color of the sky, looked at me for a moment before turning away. This should have been my chance to get away, while the human wasn't looking. The container that held me had such low sides that I might have been able to leap out of it, but my rear legs still wouldn't respond.

A strange sensation of motion began, even though the box I was in wasn't moving. My head throbbed and I hurt everywhere, so I purred to myself the way my mother would have purred to me when I wasn't feeling well. Afraid as I was, it brought me a little relief. The container amplified the sound, surrounding me with the reassuring vibrations of my own purr.

While the human was mostly doing things to make the thing on wheels go, it reached over and put its whole paw over me. I was so small that the paw covered me.

Even though humans are scary, its fingers were warm, and I shivered against them, purring to myself. I could smell things on the paw: a human smell that told me it was female, faint food odors, and the scent of other cats. Strange cats, but it still felt better to smell others of my kind. I leaned further into the human's paw, shivering and purring.

When the sense of motion stopped, the human lifted me, bin and all, and carried me into a building that smelled like many animals, especially like stinky dogs. More female humans inside exclaimed over me, "She's so tiny!"

Rescued Volume 2

Humans are scary.

There was nowhere to hide in the bin, so I cowered in the farthest corner and shivered harder until the human carried me into a room where yet another human came in to examine me. I didn't want to be handled, but I didn't feel well enough to put up a fight. I hissed once or twice, but strange humans stretched me out under a buzzing thing that hung from above before bringing me back to where the female human waited.

"Nothing's broken. Why don't you take her home and see how she does?" one of the dog-smelling humans said. "We'll talk about that eye in a few days."

"I guess we're going home, then," said the human who picked me up by the side of the road. I sat and shivered harder, unable to control myself.

The dog-smelling humans wrapped me in a dog-smelling towel and put a large, squishy thing inside with me. It made funny sloshing noises, but it was warm, and I huddled against it beneath the dog-smelling towel as they sent us on our way.

I nestled against the warmth under the towel. Was I going home, finally? My mother must have returned by now and would be wondering where I was. I would feel better when I got back to my mother. She always made me feel safe and warm from the inside.

I drifted off to sleep despite the fear and the pain. When I woke up, I could tell immediately I wasn't back with my mother. Over the dog-smell of the towels, I could smell other cats. I smelled humans, too. I was still huddled under the towel against the warm thing, and when

Ashton: A Scary Situation

I opened my one working eye, I saw a strange, black cat peering in at me.

The cat saw me open my eye and hissed. "Who are you? This is *my* house."

"Our house," another cat hissed from very nearby. My head hurt too much to lift and try to see the second cat.

"Stop it, both of you," said the female human. "Be nice to her. She's having a very bad day."

The black cat hissed again, "And that's *my* human, so don't get too many ideas about snuggling with her."

"Talia, cut it out," said a deeper voice. "You're always going to be the number one girl around here." The voice came from a second human, who leaned down and picked up the black cat. I could smell that this other human was male, and he had fur on his face as well as on top of his head, like the human who had chased me away from my family.

I cowered back under the towels, pressing against the warm thing. I was so afraid, I forgot to purr to make myself feel better.

A gray striped cat's face poked down into the gap in the towels, his whiskers brushing against me. "Our humans," hissed the gray cat.

"Enough, Pierre," said the female human, pulling the gray cat back from where I shivered under the towels. I heard her make a funny smacking noise with her mouth, and then she said, "You'll get more kisses later. Let me take care of the little one now." She scooped me up with her paws and put me into a cage with a heated pad, a litter box and a bowl of water. A cage! I was a wild cat, a free cat (if rather a small one), and I was in a cage! But my moment of outrage was overwhelmed by my throbbing head and aching back end. I couldn't do much more than curl up against the heated pad. At least it didn't smell like dogs.

I awoke some time later to see an orange cat resting his head on his paws, eyes watching me. Before I was able to blink and focus my good eye, I thought it was my brother. Then I realized this cat was much bigger and was on the other side of the cage bars that surrounded me. Now that I was fully awake, I saw that the strange cat had a broad nose and a soft-looking mane, and he lifted his head from his paws when he realized I had awakened.

"Do you want to play?" he asked hopefully. Maybe this big cat wasn't so different from my brother after all.

I raised my head a little and the world spun around me, then slowly righted. I wasn't going to be playing with anyone just yet. Besides, I played with my brother, not this huge, orange stranger.

The thought of my brother made me wonder what happened to him. Did the scary human go back to where he hid under the green leaves? I hoped he and my mother were safe.

The big cat continued to watch me. He and I both heard approaching human footsteps at the same time. He jumped up and greeted the human who entered the room with inexplicable enthusiasm. Didn't his mother teach him that humans are scary?

The human opened the cage and I wobbled backward. I watched her set down a dish of the most delicious-smelling food ever. I inched away warily, caught between

Ashton: A Scary Situation

the pang of hunger that gripped my stomach nearly as much as the pain in my head, and my fear of the human.

The human reached in faster than I could move in my woozy state, and touched me a few times. I was going to have to bathe thoroughly to get the human smell off of me! I turned to start grooming and saw that the orange cat was eating my food. With a squeak, I forgot my fear and wobbled up to eat. I stood with my front paws in the dish and gobbled it down, ignoring the human as she pulled back the orange cat and told me, "Enjoy your chicken." I didn't even look up when she closed the cage door.

That's how it continued. The orange cat was rarely far from my cage. Sometimes he scratched fiercely on the post nearby. Sometimes he napped on the furniture on the other side of the cage. Sometimes he napped on top of the cage, with his long, orange fur sticking through the bars.

I quickly learned the sound of food being prepared, even though it was done where I couldn't see it, and I would meow frantically for my bowl whenever the human brought it into the room. I wasn't missing another meal if I could help it.

The human started using the word "Ashton" whenever she talked to me. She used it with almost every single thing she said. I noticed that she used the word "Newton" in lots of things she said to the orange cat, but she never said it to me. I finally deduced that she was calling him Newton and me Ashton. It wasn't what my mother had called me, but humans can't pronounce things that cats say, so I decided it would have to do.

One day after I finished eating, I realized the cage door was still open. Free from my imprisonment at last! The human was on all fours in front of the cage, watching me. I walked out onto the hard floor. I was so happy that without thinking, I pushed the blind side of my head against the human's cheek in greeting as I passed. I don't know whether she or I was more surprised that I had done it!

I covered my confusion by trotting over to where the big, orange at was waiting expectantly for me. We had sniffed each other through the cage before, but we could give each other a thorough sniffing now.

The orange cat wiggled his big rear to tell me he wanted to play, then he whacked me with his wide paw. Surprised, I tried to whack him back and missed.

Ashton: A Scary Situation

Losing an eye meant my aim wasn't as good as it used to be when I played this game with my brother. He swatted me again, and I chased him across the room. The gray and black cats watched from the doorway, twitching their whiskers in amusement, but they didn't join the game.

When we were done chasing, instead of going back to the cage, I walked over to the big piece of furniture where the human quietly sat. It was too high to jump on, especially with my still-aching hindquarters, but a nimble kitten like me could climb instead of jumping. The surface where the human sat was incredibly soft. This was so much more comfortable than the inside of my cage! I curled up and purred. Sure, my hindquarters still ached and my head still hurt, but this was the best thing yet about being with the human. I was still purring as I fell asleep.

Just as I was starting to accept that this was going to be my life, the human took me back to the dog-smelling humans.

Humans are scary, especially dog-smelling humans.

They made me sleep and did something to my bad eye. Then they put an irritating cone around my neck so I couldn't reach my own face. It was terrible, sitting in a cage, unable to bathe the dog-smelling human smell away. Humans passed by constantly, and dogs barked and whined nearby.

If this had happened right after the human first took me, it wouldn't have been so bad. It would have been all I knew about how things can be with humans. But after spending time at the human's house where there was food twice a day and the orange cat to play with, I knew that life around humans, scary as they were, could be less scary and more comfortable than this.

I scrunched back in the cage, as far as I could get from the dog-smelling humans, but the cone around my neck kept getting in the way. I missed my mother and brother. I even missed the orange cat at the human's house.

When the female human came to rescue me from the dog-smelling humans, I was so glad to see her that I caught myself thinking, "*My* human!" when I was carried out to her. I burrowed against her neck, shivering and clinging to her. I really had thought I would never see her again and would have to spend the rest of my life with the dog-smelling humans.

She took me back to the house with the orange cat, and the first thing I did was check to be sure that my soft furniture was still there. I climbed up, and it was just as soft as I remembered. With a big sigh, I sprawled out, cone and all. I hoped I wouldn't have to leave here ever again.

After this terrible ordeal, I gradually started to feel better again. My hind end slowly mended, and finally my head stopped hurting all the time, too. My face felt strange sometimes when I bathed, and once, when I looked at the reflective door, I saw a one-eyed cat staring back. With a shock, I realized that was me. I looked funny, but felt better at last.

Part of feeling better meant I didn't need the human any more. When I was hurt and afraid, I let her near me

Ashton: A Scary Situation

and even climbed all over her a time or two. But now that I was all better, I was a wild kitten again.

The human was dismayed that I didn't want to be near her any more. Whenever I curled up on the back of the furniture that she called a sofa and she sat too close, I jumped down and ran across the room to the cat tree where Newton sharpened his claws.

"You're hurting my feelings, Ashton!" my human said. The only word I really understood was Ashton, and I blinked my one eye at her from across the room to let her know I understood she was talking to me.

But my human was as sneaky as she could be scary. She decided that if I wasn't going to let her near me except at mealtime, I was going to have to eat close to her. Not just close to her. On her!

One evening, the human came over with my bowl of food, and then she sat down on the floor and placed my dinner on her lap. I had two choices: not eat — as if I would choose that! — or eat from her lap. So I cautiously edged forward and put my front paws on her leg and took a few bites. She touched me with her those big paws of hers while I was eating, but I was too hungry to run away. The whole thing was really undignified, but hungry always won out over human-scary. As soon as I was done eating, I scooted away from her touchy-feely paws, and I mostly kept my distance from her after that until the next mealtime — and she repeated the whole routine again. And again and again, at every mealtime from then on.

I confess, after a while I let the human touch me sometimes between meals. But I only allowed it when it was my idea, like when I was at the top of the cat tree, where I felt secure. I could tell by the tone of her voice that touching me made my human happy, but I could only let her do so much of it before it became too scary and I had to hide.

After the moon outside the windows had grown full and small and full again, I grew too big to eat from the human's lap. The bowl and I didn't both fit in her lap any more, and she stopped feeding me there. It was a relief to be able to eat like a big cat, with my bowl on the floor, but I kind of missed having her stroke me with her paws while I was eating. Not that I would have admitted that, even to my friend the orange cat.

Time passed. I wondered whether my mother and my brother were all right and if they would recognize me now that I was a mostly-grown cat. One day, the black cat who had hissed at me when I first arrived went away to the dog-smelling humans and never came back. My human came home without him, her shoulders drooping and her eyes downcast. Even though humans express their sadness differently than we cats do, I could still tell what she was feeling. At night, especially, water leaked from her eyes. The black cat had slept in the bed with her while the rest of us cats slept other places around the house, and now that the black cat was gone, my human was lonely for a cat in the bed.

My human did everything she could think of to make the bed more inviting for us cats, but none of us wanted to sleep there. The gray cat liked to sleep on the chair. The orange cat usually slept on the living room sofa.

Ashton: A Scary Situation

I slept on the sunroom's sofa where I always had. I was tempted to join my human on the bed when I could tell she was sad, but the male human was there, too, and he was still much too scary for me to approach.

Sometimes the male human wasn't home at the time my human went to bed. On those nights, I would circle closer toward the bed in the darkened room, my paws padding quietly on the wood floor. I knew from exploring the bed in the daytime that it was soft like the sofa, so I didn't blame the human for wanting to sleep there. It could be cozy to share, if it wasn't so scary.

One night when the male human was away and my human seemed especially sad, I circled the bed on the floor as usual. I heard the human sniffle sadly, and I remembered how I could tell she was happy when she touched me. Not giving myself time to stop and think too long about it, I wiggled my rear and jumped lightly up onto the bed. My human must have felt me land beside her feet, because she froze in place, hardly breathing.

I walked up and down between her and the edge of the bed. This was scary. *Humans are scary.* But it wasn't too bad so far. If it got any scarier, I could easily slip right off the edge of the bed. I walked halfway back up the bed and kneaded against my human's side.

Her breath hitched once or twice when my claws caught her, but she was silent and still. This was not too scary yet. Carefully, I turned around twice the way my mother taught me before curling up against the human's hip, my toes close to the edge of the bed in case I needed a quick getaway.

Rescued Volume 2

Slowly, ever so slowly, my human lowered her big paw to rest on my flank, softly against my stripes. I flinched a little when she first touched me, and we both tensed up. I flexed my claws against the bed, ready to bolt away. But she didn't grab me or hold me down, and I could hear that she wasn't making any more sad noises.

Then she gave a little sigh, a breathy sound of air escaping. I sighed, too, and my claws released the bed as I lowered my head to rest on my forepaws. An unexpected warmth spread through me from the inside, like the feeling I used to have when I was with my mother. I began to purr and closed my eyes.

Humans are scary, but maybe not my human.

Piggy: The Claw Machine Cat

My love affair with food is somewhat of a running joke, but I take it all in good-natured fun. If I can make a few people laugh, I'm making a difference. It hasn't always been this way. I'm here to tell you about a time before the human, Matt, became my new daddy. A time most cats wouldn't want to think about.

🐾 🐾 🐾

Sunshine filters through the screened window, warming my whiskers. I look over at Matt, blinking in the slow, lazy way cats do, showing him how much I adore him. I watch him at his most favorite of pastimes: working at the computer. My adopted sister cat, Goober, runs amok — sliding on the hardwood

Rescued Volume 2

floors, enthralled by a squeaky feather toy, which has long since been silenced. She's a whirlwind of tiger-striped fur, young and vibrant. I'm a bit older, and more settled.

Goober jumps onto the windowsill gently prodding me with her paw — her invitation to playtime. I look away. *Not now little sister.* I have more serious thoughts on my mind.

Last night, Matt found old paperwork while digging through a filing cabinet in his room. I watched several emotions cross his face as he studied the documents: sadness, and then anger.

"These are your adoption papers," he said to me. I peered over his shoulder and saw an old black and white photo of a cat looking back at me. I realized this was me a long time ago. "Muffin." I hardly remember the name and a shiver runs through me. I was so thin at the time. *Thin, neglected, and abandoned.* Another memory comes to mind, one I don't linger on too long: a hand raised in anger toward me.

Many years have separated me from that time. Years, and the love of one good man, my human, Matt. This moment is one of sweet, twittering birdies, crunchy tuna treats, and a fluffy, warm bed. I am a cat who is fortunate indeed.

"Piggy!" Matt calls out, and I shake myself back into the present. "Piggy, look," Matt says as he points to the computer screen. "You have over eighteen-thousand 'Likes' on your Facebook page. That's quite an accomplishment." He walks over to me and scoops me from my perch, petting my head and scratching *the* spot

Piggy: The Claw Machine Cat

behind my ears. Purr...my tail goes limp, paws tingling with ecstasy. Oh purrrr!

Eighteen-thousand. Not bad for a cat who was once unwanted.

Matt sits back down, cradling me like a baby, and I snuggle into the familiar scent of his sweatshirt, safe in his arms. Goober crawls underneath the computer chair, tickling Matt's legs with her paws. He bends to pet her with the hand that's not supporting me, while the contented sound of my purring warms the silence of the room.

"You're a Facebook diva," Matt says, scrolling through the photos on my page. I have no idea what these words mean, but I consider them compliments because the smile on his face is huge and his happiness evident. Picture after picture of such good memories: Matt and me making funny faces after a morning of play. Catnip-induced smirks upon the faces of my sister and I after a romp with new toy mice. My paw dipping into a dessert Matt left at his computer. Our little family.

I drift toward sleep, content on my human's lap, but the name Muffin once again comes to mind. And when sleep overtakes me, dreams and memories take me along with them.

The little girl found me shivering outside her house. Alone and frightened, I'd wandered out of the woods, still confused from the recent events that had led me there. Only a week before, I'd lost my human companion, the kindly old man who'd brought me into his home and then into his heart. His grown children had shown up one day and taken him from me. They said he wasn't fit to live alone any longer.

One of them tried approaching me, and I'd bolted straight out the front door and into the woods behind the house. That's where I watched and waited, scared and confused, hoping my companion would return. And when days had gone by with no sign of him, I resigned myself to the fact that I'd never see him again.

The little girl approached me and then picked me up. "Ooh, another kitty," she squealed. "Velvet's gonna love you." The child, grimy from many days' worth of dirt, brought me into her home. A place of utter chaos, a place where I would learn that the sting of a raised hand meant business.

I trembled, huddling in the corner of a damp, musty basement, the feel of cold cement underneath the pads of my paws. I had run to the sanctuary of the lowest level to escape the deafening sounds of the humans. A fight had broken out between the man and woman once again, and I knew to steer clear of them during these times.

I lay there looking over at the other cat, Velvet, who'd been my companion, my sister through it all. She laid her head onto her paws and sighed, closing her eyes as if blocking out the tumult above.

My belly rumbled with hunger, and I crept forward to poke my paw at the upended plastic water bowl.

Piggy: The Claw Machine Cat

Our food dish, an antique china saucer laid broken in two with the remnants of our last meal crusted on the edges.

Velvet looked up, her eyes huge and sad. I couldn't remember the last time we'd eaten. I knew she was hungry too, and I wished there was something I could do to comfort her. She counted on me and I'd become her protector, motherly when she needed it most.

Sludgy water trickled slowly into a drain on the basement floor from a leak in the old washtubs. I moved forward to the puddle, lapped up the filthy liquid, and then retched it right back up.

I joined Velvet, curling next to her soft coat, and we both fell into fitful slumber.

When I awoke the next morning, I noticed there weren't the usual cacophony of morning sounds. The humans were silent.

Weak from hunger and thirst, I could barely move. Velvet looked at me, sleepy eyes filled with questions.

I waited and still heard nothing. Curiosity got the better of me, and with the last of my strength, I mounted the rickety staircase, leaving Velvet behind. What I saw in the rooms above made my fur stand on end. The house stood in complete disarray. No sign of any of the humans. Closet doors stood open and empty.

They left us? I took a moment to process this thought. *Surely someone will be back.* I remembered talk of the woman threatening to leave the man and take all those kids with her.

I walked through the remainder of the place Velvet and I called home. Poking my whiskers into bedrooms, slithering into open closets, I could find nothing that gave a clue to what had gone on.

Back in the kitchen, I hopped onto the counter and found a skillet of cold, congealed bacon sitting on top of the stove. I called to Velvet and we both picked at the old, tasteless meal. Afterward, we washed each other's coats, and then curled together on the threadbare rug in the corner of the kitchen.

Several days went by with no sign of the family we'd lived with. I'd known fear before, but nothing had come close to the realization that hunger brought. My stomach rumbled constantly, and Velvet began to look thin and sickly. Looking to the sky one evening as I sat on the windowsill of the living room, I closed my eyes with a wish and a prayer and then fell into a dreamless sleep.

A rap at the living room window the next morning woke me, and the puzzled face of the mail carrier peered into the house. I heard him call out, "Hello, is anyone there?" I stretched out, reached up and scratched at the grimy glass with my paws startling him. "My goodness, are you alone in there, kitty?"

I yowled, scratching at the glass more feverishly. *Come on mister, what's it going to take? A neon sign perhaps?*

A few hours later, Velvet and I were scooped into cat carriers — something I still can't abide to this day — and escorted from the place we'd once called home. The mail carrier took us to a veterinarian's office. I heard him telling the girl at the front desk, "You shoulda seen the filth in that home. Stuff everywhere and not a drop of food or water for these two poor cats."

Piggy: The Claw Machine Cat

The days went by in a blur, with doctors and nurses poking and prodding us, but there was plenty to eat and drink, and no shortage of cat kibble and fresh water.

When our health improved, we were taken to a shelter, Animal Friends, with a big sign on our cage: *Must be adopted together.* I'd heard the vet and his assistant talking one day: "These two can't be separated especially after all they've been through with each other."

Animal Friends was full of surprises. I'd never been around so many different varieties of cats, but there were other animals as well. Guinea Pigs squeaked in their cages, showing off their portly little bodies and whimsical skills. Bunnies scampered around their pen, their fluffy little cottontails wiggling. The dogs were the most annoying of all. I didn't care for the constant yap-yap-yap of the wiry terrier nearby. When nobody else was looking, I let loose my best snake-like hiss to try and scare the "yip" right out of him, but to no avail.

A parade of people came and went, some pausing longer than others to look at me and Velvet. Hands poked into our cage — little kids with sticky-sweet fingers that smelled good enough to lick, and others that carried the scent of their own pets which I shied away from. Nobody appealed to me.

A big man with a kind voice came by one day. He spoke softly to me and Velvet, and took time to read our sign. I heard him muttering something under his breath about misfits and rejection. When he reached into our cage, he stroked me gently, doing the same with my sister. All the while he kept talking to us, telling us what nice kitties we were. It didn't take him long to call the clerk over to let him know he wanted us. He could have picked Fiona, the prissy gray cat with the luxurious fur, or Sadie, the fetching blue-eyed Siamese. Surely there were many other cats there with gorgeous coats and darling personalities. I wasn't a stunning cat. As a domestic shorthair I'd always felt quite ordinary. I was shy and a little backward from all I'd gone through. But this man had seen something in me, something beautiful and valuable.

Of course I couldn't help but wonder if he might be like the others. Could we trust him? And if I liked him, would he also be taken from me as my first human companion had been?

The man turned out to be Matt's Uncle Rick, who'd been looking for two cats to adopt. Since he worked with special needs children, he knew a thing or two about kindness and patience. He took us to a cozy home that night, and it was there I met Matt, his nephew, a skinny fellow with a warm smile.

The two of them stood looking at me and Velvet, plying us with tasty food, fresh water and an assortment of cat toys.

"I think the first thing we'll do, is to re-name you girls," Rick said.

He pointed to Velvet. "Your gray coat reminds me of a comic book character I always liked. I think we'll call you The Vision." Velvet blinked her golden eyes in response and sidled up to Rick.

"Now you," he said, indicating me, "I'm not so sure yet. Let's see if a name presents itself. How does that sound?"

Piggy: The Claw Machine Cat

I didn't care. Call me anything you want, but please don't call me late for dinner! I had developed a very fond relationship with food. I couldn't get enough. Bowls in this house were always filled to the brim with tuna cat chow. Treats were even more wonderful. When one of the humans took the treat bag off the counter, the crinkly sound would send me into spasms of kitty ecstasy.

Two weeks went by. Rick and Matt spent time with "Vision" the cat and me. Rick peered at me thoughtfully, a smirk lighting up his eyes.

"Well, I believe we've come up with a name for you, he said, patting my head and stifling a chuckle. "I think we'll call you Piggy. You have a pink pig nose, and well, er, you seem to have gained quite a bit of weight already."

Piggy indeed! Well, if that's what they wanted to call me, fine. Just keep the food and snacks coming, my friends, and I'd answer to anything.

Life settled into a pleasurable routine with these two young men. I enjoyed venturing into nooks and crannies in my new home. That is when I found that I bonded the most with Matt. His bedroom was in the basement, a small, low-lit room. I liked the cozy feeling in there, but mostly I liked Matt. He was a good sort, always in a happy mood with a nice, smiling face. He took extra time to cuddle with me or play, laughing whenever I did something he found amusing. Who knew that dipping my paw into the popcorn kernels in his snack bowl could be so funny or that his shoelaces would provide hours of entertainment for us both? Or that the paperwork he sometimes laid on his bed and the sound when I attacked it would be so hilarious to him? He was studying video editing and he began shooting videos of me and my antics.

Nighttime was my favorite — the soft blankets on Matt's bed, our special snuggle time, and hearing Matt talk about his hopes and dreams for the future. I could listen to him for hours, falling asleep in the crook of his arm.

A couple of years flew by, and Vision and I were as content as cats could be. Something bothered me though. Vision had begun to lose weight once again. The spark in her eyes began to dim, and she slept more than ever. It was about this time that Matt took her to the veterinary clinic. They returned home a little quiet. Vision curled under our dining room table, unable to move, and hardly able to eat. I tried enticing her to play. I lay by her side, hoping she'd snap out of whatever was bothering her, but after a few weeks, I saw Matt take Vision away again. This time she never returned.

We'd been a team, inseparable. I wanted her back. I missed the lovely velvet cat I'd come to know as my sister. We'd been through so much together and now she was gone. With my heart broken, I reached out to Matt for comfort during this time, completely trusting him.

🐾 🐾 🐾

I awake, shaking myself from the long dream and memories, clearing my head. Matt gets up from his computer chair and lays me on his bed. Goober runs between his legs, making that little trilling sound when

Piggy: The Claw Machine Cat

she wants to play. Matt chases her around the room while I sit watching them. Sticking my toes into the air, I begin licking my glorious white fur, extra careful to clean between the pads of my paws. Goober flies onto the bed, and I lay a paw over her back, pinning her down. I run my sandpaper tongue over my paw and wash cobwebs and dust from my adopted sister's coat. Who knows where she's been — perhaps in the basement behind the furnace, poking her whiskers into places she shouldn't. Little by little, Goober relaxes and begins to drift off to sleep, a content cat smile on her face as she relishes my grooming.

I glance over at Matt's computer screen, stifling a kitty chuckle. It's not easy being known as a Facebook diva and opinionated puss. It takes work, lots of work. Matt still films me, but in the last several years, he's been filming himself too. He's become a YouTube celebrity! His years of video editing and camera skills have paid off. Matt makes family-friendly arcade videos for children and their parents. He plays what he calls "claw machines" also known as crane games. You see them in arcades in malls and amusement parks — the big glass-encased games lit all the way around with sparkly lights, playing silly music and stuffed with prizes and plush toys. Matt purchased his own machine, and well, I will get to that in just a moment.

Matt and I moved out about a year after Vision went to the place that humans call the Rainbow Bridge. He'd grown older and wanted a home of his own. Although Uncle Rick had been wonderful, and we were both grateful for all he'd done, there was never a question where my loyalty lay. I was Matt's cat now and would be going with him.

The new house had even more rooms to explore and lots of windows with a panorama of outdoor activity for me to watch. Birds flitted from branch to branch in tall trees and then flew away, filling the air with songs. Colorful butterflies and striped honeybees floated past, their erratic patterns almost dizzying. I sat on the windowsill in Matt's room for hours, late into the night, amused by all that nature offered.

The day the first arcade machine arrived, I thought Matt would burst with joy. An enormous truck pulled up in front of our home. I watched from the bedroom window as he greeted the man who got out of it. After signing several papers, they loaded a huge piece of equipment onto a wheeled dolly. I heard our front door open, and then hid under the bed for hours to escape the racket they made while they brought that contraption into the house. Later, when I emerged, curious and brave, I crept down the stairs to our game room and saw it. Matt shined the glass, tinkered with the electronic coin mechanism, and then loaded boxes full of small stuffed animals into the machine. He practiced on it for hours while I watched him, honestly a little indifferent to the whole thing.

"Piggy, this is our future," he told me.

I gave him a look. *I don't care about the future, Matt, just remember the present. I'm on a strict schedule here. It's suppertime, pal.*

Matt sat watching me. He asked if I was happy. I rubbed in and out of his legs revving up my best purr,

Piggy: The Claw Machine Cat

hoping this would be the answer he needed. He told me there would be a surprise for me now since I'd been such a good girl. It would arrive in a few days. I loved surprises since they were usually in the form of a new toy, blanket, or tasty treat, so I waited with anticipation.

The big day arrived. Matt walked into the living room with a cardboard box. I sniffed the air, my delicate nose working, when an unusual scent caught my attention. The box began to meow and Matt lifted a tiny grey-striped kitten from it. I backed up and hissed. *Uh, Matt, if this is the surprise, then I think I'd rather not.*

The new kitten was rambunctious and playful. I can't say I liked her much at first. But Matt knew me better than I knew myself. He'd sensed my loneliness, and had seen how I thrived when I had another cat to look after — how motherly I'd always been. We named the kitten Goober, which is another name for little peanut.

Matt's YouTube popularity began picking up more and more. Families everywhere watched Matt's videos, even those living in other countries. He taught excellent tips on winning at the claw machines and other games, and with his fun, quirky personality, the people loved him. He filmed me and Goober too, always luring us to the camera with some zany stunt.

Fan mail and little gifts began pouring in. Kids would send drawings of the prizes they won. Nothing was better, however, than when the fan mail began to come for me! Little toys, drawings, and occasional bags of cat treats started to arrive. Matt decided to create a Facebook page for me, and his mom, Karen, who is a writer, started to post my thoughts and photos of my antics daily.

It's fun interacting with all the comments on my page. I like making people laugh, and have developed a quirky cat persona as a food connoisseur. I am not opposed to a little humor regarding my girlish figure either. Many gentleman cats have tried courting me and approve of the way I look. I am living proof a girl doesn't have to have the perfect shape to have a slew of tomcats at her doorstep. I like a good meal, and I'm not afraid to talk about it.

I enjoy humor most of all, and have penned a few poems in my day. I'd like to share my most popular one with you called "Piggy's Ode to Food":

> *Today I'm not quite in the mood,*
> *May I just have a little food?*
> *A little treat to tide me over,*
> *A little snack for me and Rover.*
> *Hey, I mentioned a dog, but we don't have one,*
> *Oh well, why not, he'd be such fun.*
> *I wouldn't care who came over today,*
> *I'd share my food, we'd laugh and play.*

Piggy: The Claw Machine Cat

So human, please don't make me sick,
Get me some treats, and be real quick.
You take too long, this cat is done.
So hop to it now, to the kitchen, run!
I'm waiting here with bated breath,
I'll fall over and starve to death.
Some crunchies please and I'll stop whining,
I'll sit at the table and I'll be dining.
Okay, enough, as you see I'm tired,
I've written too much and now I'm wired.
I'll let you know when it's time to eat,
Peace out, phew...now, this cat is beat.

There's so much seriousness in this hurting world. Matt and I like to think that if we can brighten just one day or at least a few hours for a child or her family, then we are doing something worthwhile.

🐾 🐾 🐾

The house is quiet, nighttime has fallen. Matt turns on the small lamps and nightlights in each room and a cozy glow surrounds us. We are in the living room now, and Matt settles into an overstuffed chair, his new video game system on his lap. Goober is washing, gliding a slender tiger paw over her face while I look over Matt's shoulder, watching a computer screen where colorful cartoonish figures jump around a make believe landscape.

Matt shakes the treat bag sitting next to him, and Goober stops. Her little head pops up and she makes that cute cooing sound. I instantly come alert and meow my loudest just to be sure Matt doesn't pass me by.

I know better, really. I am treated like a special princess. I think about the less fortunate cats in the world, ones I see on other Facebook pages in the cat community. The ferals, blind cats, three-legged cats, and I pause to give a moment of thankfulness for who I am and where I am in this moment in time. Once neglected, abandoned, and unloved, I cannot help but feel gratitude for the circumstances that have led me on my journey.

I still miss my sister Vision, but I know I'll see her again someday at the Rainbow Bridge. There, we will frolic and play and the tuna will flow freely. There, we will be reunited with other loved ones; our momma cats who we don't even remember now, and our litter sisters and brothers.

As I crunch into the treat, I look into Matt's eyes. What I see warms me to the tip of my pink Piggy nose. I see true, unconditional love.

Jazmine's Story...by Mr. Jazz

I realize this is a bit unconventional, considering this story really isn't about me at all and I've long since passed on, but if you'll allow me the courtesy of continuing, you'll actually see it is. Call it fate, destiny, kismet, magic — I like to think of it as spiritual intervention — but if it weren't for me and my meddling ways, a certain orange rescue kitten, my namesake, would have never found her true purpose.

Let me introduce myself — my name is Mr. Jazz — I'm a Ragdoll cat, or I was when I was here on earth. On August 28, 2013, after 15 years of life, I asked my beloved humans for the most difficult gift of all — to help me cross the Rainbow Bridge. I wrote a book about my life and death experiences, *Purr Prints of the Heart — A Cat's Tale of Life, Death, and Beyond*, but my afterlife is where the true story begins.

Rescued Volume 2

It all started rather haphazardly. I don't like to meow disrespectfully of my humans — after all they did provide me with 15 wonderful years of food, loving, toys, and everything a cat could ever need or want. But truth be told, in grieving me, they had lost that spark that gives life its meaning. And along with their broken hearts, they had some personal issues making them cranky — you know, kind of like how we kitties get when the cat carrier comes out of hiding for a trip to the vet. Anymeow, Mom, as I called my female human, was in her office at the time preparing some marketing materials for a pet expo she was scheduled to attend when *it* happened.

It. Sorry — let me back up so this makes more sense to you. First off, you need to know my Mom is all about that fate, destiny, kismet, and magic thing I was telling you about. Like *seriously* about it. Some of you might sneeze at that, and honestly I might have myself at one point, were it not for the fact I'm here for that *very* reason.

I won't bore you with the whole story; let's just say that many, many years ago — back when Mom was practically a prehistoric saber-toothed cat and long before I was even a thought in her head, she was cleaning the house. Normally she didn't turn the TV on while cleaning, but on this particular day *she did.* The first thing that popped on the screen was a show on Animal Planet about cat breeds — in particular, the Ragdoll.

Mom had never heard of the Ragdoll before and instantly fell in love with our sweet faces and beautiful chocolate and cream-colored fur coats. She wanted one

Jazmine's Story...by Mr. Jazz

of us that very moment. After hunting down an ad in the newspaper (yes, it was that long ago), she convinced her two boys to adopt me as a Mother's Day gift for her. They all drove several hours to get me, but when they got to the breeder's house; the breeder had the nerve to tell Mom to adopt one of my siblings instead of me because I was sickly. Mom didn't care — she loved me just the way I was and defiantly took me home. So had Mom not turned the TV on that very moment, I wouldn't have been a part of her life, meaning there would be no namesake and you wouldn't be reading this chapter.

The other thing about Mom is that she is practically a cat herself — not only does she regularly wear cat ears as a fashion statement (yes, you read that right), she's also a cat advocate, award-winning cat blogger, and cat author. Her passion is educating people, especially about the need for spay and neuter to help reduce the astounding numbers of cats living on the streets and in shelters. She didn't know about all that stuff when she brought me home, but as she got older she learned, and she went to all kinds of pet related events to meet people and to find out more ways to help cats so that she could write about it.

What really matters is that on *this* particular evening, as she was getting ready for this pet expo, I could sense something was wrong. Normally Mom looked forward to these types of events — another opportunity to wear those cat ears! Plus this time my human male, Dad, would be going with her. Since it was only a couple hours drive, they were going together. Dad had never met Mom's cat buddies, so it was a big deal. And Dad's human Mom (aka Nana) lived near the expo center, so they were going to extend their trip to visit her. Everything was squared away with my catmates at home — Zee, Zoey, Harley, Mia, Peanut, Rolz, and Kizmet. Mom's mom was going to cat-sit. So why was she question-

ing the whole thing? Why didn't she want to go?

Being a spirit was relatively new to me so I wasn't sure how it all worked, but *something* was telling me she HAD to go and I needed to paw in. Normally when I would "visit" Mom after my trip to the Rainbow Bridge, I would be subtle because I didn't want to spook her. Mostly I would just look at her from down the hallway at night when she was on the couch watching TV, or come lie on her feet when she went to bed at night. I was pretty sure she knew it was me, but I wasn't completely convinced because sometimes I felt she thought she was imagining me because she missed me so much.

Anymeow, this required drastic measures so I went directly to Mom's office and stood in her doorway. I didn't care if I scared her — I needed her to see me. She looked up from what she was doing and our eyes locked. My heart broke as I looked at her and I chocked back a tear. It was worse than I imagined — her once bright eyes full

Jazmine's Story...by Mr. Jazz

of life and possibility were a listless, hollow, and dull pool of hopelessness. She had lost her way and I couldn't let that happen.

"Go," I gently whispered to her.

Neither of us understood the full implication of my visitation at the time but somehow it was enough. She finished up for the day and when she came to sit on the couch, this time I came and sat on her tummy like I did when I was alive. She felt my weight on her body and reached her hand out to pet me — it was a beautiful moment and I knew it was her way of letting me know that she trusted my instinct and that she would go.

The next day Mom and Dad headed for the expo. Despite my intervention, the energy between them was strained during the ride. Between my passing and other personal issues, they were a forlorn bundle of depressed nerves, like a grey scribble crayon cloud was following them. I started to get nervous. Had I made a mistake getting involved? I tried to put it out of my mind as they got out of the car and ventured into the massive exhibit hall.

Oh My Cat! The exhibit area was a fast-paced, crowded clowder of people, exhibitors, retailers, bloggers, writers, media, veterinarians, and celebrities, all hawking their wares. Everywhere you looked there were mountains of stuff for every creature imaginable! But the cat stuff — *meow*! Cat condos reaching to the sky, endless rows of every tempting cat toy on earth, cat totes, cat carriers, cat food, cat bowls, cat clothes, and more! There was even a really cool display — a larger than life-sized cardboard cutout of a super cute orange kitten that people posed with for photos. When Mom and some of her blogging friends had their pictures taken by the display, one of them mentioned that the cutout reminded her of a ginger Maine Coon-like kitten she had just seen at one of the exhibit booths.

Silly Mom barely heard the comment about the kitten and didn't give it another thought. Typically if she knew a kitten was anywhere nearby, she would drop whatever she was doing to go see it. In her world, kittens trump all else — even chocolate, shoes, books, and coffee. Especially if that kitten might be a Maine Coon or Maine Coon mix because Mom and Dad *love* these big, fluffy cats. In fact, two of my cat-mates were Maine Coons — Zee and Kizmet. But Mom was still feeling blue. She was tired, and sad, and overwhelmed, and she just wanted to go home and take a catnap. There was one day left to the expo, but I could tell her heart wasn't in it.

I was puzzled and getting more anxious by the minute. Why did I convince Mom to go to the expo if there was no reason for it? Nothing magical had happened so far. No life-changing events, just a lot of really cool cat stuff to look at.

"Please Mom," I purred in her ear, my paws crossed that my premonition would come true. "Stay strong — I just *know* there is a reason you are here."

The paw crossing must have worked because they stayed the night and when Mom woke up, rather than putting on her old, ratty sweatpants — a sure sign she was preparing for an early ride home — she showered and put on a respectable outfit, including her

Jazmine's Story...by Mr. Jazz

trademark cat ears! After a morale-boosting cup of coffee, she and Dad made it to the expo and did the best they could to get through the day before they headed out to visit Nana. Mom had one last meeting scheduled for the end of the day with someone at Imperial Cat, a company that makes high quality, corrugated cat scratchers. She was debating whether she should go, or just cancel so she and Dad could hit the road to Nana's a bit earlier.

At this point I was feeling like a feline failure. But even in her depressed state of mind, I should have given Mom more credit — she was brought up well and proper etiquette ultimately made the decision for her. It would have been flat-out rude and unprofessional of her to cancel, so she decided to show up for her scheduled appointment.

Mom and Dad headed over to the Imperial Cat booth, but the person she was supposed to meet with wasn't there. It was some sort of time mix-up, but who was there, but *her* — her being an impossibly adorable ginger kitten, the spitting image of a Maine Coon, sitting on a throne-shaped cat scratcher like royalty. Her white bib and mittens gave her a touch of elegance as she held court amid the loud roar of the crowd. It was the very same kitten Mom's friend had told her about, the one that looked like the cat in front of the exhibit area where Mom had her picture taken. Are you getting chills yet?

So here was this kitten — bold, sassy, confident, stunning, and charming, rolled up into one fantastically fabulous, diva-licious ball of ginger kitten fuzz.

She looked squarely at Mom and Dad with her glowing amber eyes and impatiently mewed:

"It's about time. I've been waiting all day for you two sad sacks. The expo's about to close. Now hurry up and fall in love with me — you know you can't resist."

Mom and Dad had a million questions first. What was her name? Where did she come from? Why was she at the expo? The young woman staffing the booth shared what little information she knew. She didn't even know if she had a name. They decided to call her Empress because she looked like royalty, sitting on their throne-shaped scratcher. She believed Empress was a stray kitten that had found her way into the barn of an abandoned farmhouse. The farmhouse owner had died and the property was overrun with feral cats, goats, and cows. A rescue organization, Florida Little Dog Rescue, found her and then placed her with a foster family to help socialize her. The young woman did not know exactly how Empress went from the foster family to the Imperial booth, but she did know that if anyone

Jazmine's Story...by Mr. Jazz

wanted to adopt her, all the adoption fees would be paid for by Imperial.

Sniff Sorry. No matter how many times I hear it, her story always gets to me. *Abandoned at a farmhouse barn with no one to take care of her or feed her?* Awful, just awful. Anymeow, it boggled Mom and Dad's minds that there was not a line a mile long to adopt this precious being, and they were horrified to think she might have to live the rest of her life in a shelter, or worse yet... *shudder* you know....

You see it, don't you? Empress simply had to go home with Mom and Dad! I felt like the weight of the world had been lifted from me — everything started to make sense. So what was the problem now? Even with Empress putting a bewitching spell on Mom with her ginger fairy dust magic, Mom was babbling about the fact they were not prepared to bring a kitten home. They had nothing with them — food, litter, cat carrier, etc. — not to mention, they were heading to visit Nana for an overnighter and she was not a cat person. (How is that even possible?)

And what about the seven cats at home? Were they at the right stage of their lives to accept a new cat-mate? Mom wasn't so sure. Right now everything was perfect — no fighting, no litter issues. Did she want to put that dynamic in jeopardy with a kitten, even an over-the-top adorable one? Ugh! She was exhausting me with her excuses and being a real downer with her logical side. Honestly, I sensed she was still reeling from my death and felt guilty even entertaining the idea of getting another cat "so soon" to replace me.

Rescued Volume 2

For cat's sake, notwithstanding the occasional spiritual visit, I had been gone for over 6 months. I knew she loved me and it never entered my mind this kitten would be "replacing" me. I'm firmly believe the human heart has endless room when it comes to love. I would never want Mom to be afraid to feel love again — there are so many animals in rescues that deserve a chance for a happy life. Empress was one of them.

"Please hear me Mom," I whispered in her ear, "I promise if you adopt her, it won't dilute the love you had for me. Quite the opposite — it will fill my heart with joy knowing you have given another creature a chance for a happy life."

But it was Dad who finally convinced her. She watched as he crooned words of endearment to Empress, and his face softened as he nuzzled her peachy fur. It was the first time in months Mom had seen him smile. Empress had stolen his heart and he was human putty in her captivating paws. Speaking of paws, her back left one even had a tiny patch of ginger fur that was heart shaped — prophetic symbolism, I think, that it was meant to be. It was a losing battle and Mom knew it. She also sensed deep in her own heart this little ginger princess was sent to them as a symbol of rebirth and new beginnings. Yes, they were rescuing her, but even more so, *she was rescuing them.*

Without thinking twice, Mom and Dad asked the people at Imperial to get the adoption papers in order. Empress was going home with them. Everything else fell into place like a well-cleaned litter box. News that a "famous" blogger was going to adopt Empress swept

Jazmine's Story...by Mr. Jazz

throughout the expo center...an expo center that was conveniently equipped with everything necessary to properly ensure that one tiny little kitten survived a car ride with two fanatical cat lovers and an overnight stay with Nana.

Toys, food, litter, litter box, and a cat carrier — all were cheerfully donated. Empress even got her throne from Imperial Cat to take home. There was literally not a single thing that wasn't taken care of and Mom and Dad were beaming like proud new parents as they left the expo center with their little orange bundle of joy in tow.

Empress spent the car ride, content in her fancy new carrier resting on Mom's lap — unzipped so she could pet her. There was not even one meow of protest — just a lot of "I love you" slow blinks in between all the petting. Mom was used to bloodcurdling screams from most of us kitties when we traveled in the car, so this was a welcome treat and a sign of good things to come.

Mom spent most of the ride thinking of a new name for the kitten. While Empress was fitting — she certainly was treated like royalty — it just didn't have the personal appeal Mom wanted. Since the beginning of time, Mom has *always* named the pets in our family and the name had to perfectly suit our personalities, our colorings, or something that just felt right to Mom.

We currently had the "z" thing going on in our house — Zee and Zoey were our love story cats and they were also the stars of Mom's blog — *Zee & Zoey's Cat Chronicles*, so incorporating the letter "z" into a name was something Mom liked to do. Most recently was the time Mom went to Pet Supermarket — but here's the catch — *it was not her regular store.* It was a location she had never been to before. She stopped on her way home from work because we had run out of the special food she needed for our dinner. Inside the store, she was hopelessly drawn to a rescue kitten in a cage, staring into the very depths of her soul, beckoning her to take him home. Naturally, she did.

Fate and destiny. You *do* remember that about Mom, right? She named him Kizmet, as in kismet, but spelled with "z" instead of "s." So in that spirit, perhaps Empress could have become Emprezz, but no, that wasn't quite right. The traditional "z" names weren't much better: Zeena. Zenith…no and no. Not pretty or special enough. And while they are perfectly fine names, Mom didn't want the standard ginger colored names like Peaches or Sunshine either. I knew she'd come up with something eventually, but Empress/Not Empress remained nameless by the time they arrived at the not cat-loving Nana's house.

Hold your paws. Someone doesn't like cats? I believe it's Cat Rule #4.7AR, subsection qz.829 that states if someone says they don't like us; we *must* make it our mission to prove otherwise. And Empress/Not Empress was a natural. As soon as they got to Nana's house and Empress/Not Empress was let out of her carrier, she languorously stretched her exquisitely formed ginger body and chirped a beguiling "hello" meow. The rest was history — Nana was hooked.

The remainder of Empress/Not Empress's stay was spent entertaining everyone with her kitten antics, and

Jazmine's Story...by Mr. Jazz

if she was nervous, she certainly didn't let on. She played fetch with her plush mouse, she trilled, she purred, she rolled on her back to expose her fluffy belly, and when it was time for bed, she slept with Mom and Dad, tucked between them without a care in the word, as if she had been part of their life forever and ever.

Despite all that, I was nervous about her trip home. The excitement was bound to catch up with her. She had gone from a feral kitten on an abandoned farm, to living with a foster family, and then sent to a noisy convention center to be gawked at by crowds of people all day long. As if that wasn't enough, she just spent a night at a converted non-cat lover's house and now she was heading to an unfamiliar new home where she wasn't likely to be welcomed with open paws by the residing seven cats.

But there was no turning back. When they got home Mom took the carrier containing Empress/Not Empress to the guest room and quickly shut the door before the trail of seven cats following her caught whiff of what was going on. Since nothing had been prepared for Empress/Not Empress's arrival, getting things in order was Mom's first priority. The guest room happened to be the same place Kizmet called home as a kitten until he was ready to be introduced to his feline catmates and it was also the same room where I spent my final moments until my trip to the vet and my subsequent voyage to the Rainbow Bridge. The aura of past, present and future swirled around in this room like afternoon sunbeams giving way to the endless mysteries and possibilities of the night. It was the perfect place for

Empress/Not Empress to soak in the atmosphere of her new home.

Mom's a pro when it comes to bringing new kitties into her house, what with having about a hundred-million years of experience. Before you could say catnip; she had a litter box set up, and scratching posts, toys, and food all in place. Empress/Not Empress had a castle befitting a spoiled princess, complete with her very own window that had a purr-fect view of squirrel and bird TV. Mom and Dad doted on her every wish and could barely tear themselves away from her for even a minute. *Everything* she did was adorable.

"Did you see how she looked at me?" Dad would say, as if she were the only kitten on earth that ever looked at its human with eyes that could melt an iceberg.

She certainly had Mom and Dad smiling which made me happy — I had not seen them like this in ages, and I was beginning to think I never would. The kitten's sunny mood was only spoiled by the occasional smell of feline interlopers on the other side of the door — then she would hiss her displeasure. Mom wasn't too worried about it, since she had planned on gradually introducing her to the household, the way she knew careful cat parents should. She called it the "acclimation period," and in theory it was a great idea.

But Kizmet — about a year and a half old then — had plans of his own. Empress/Not Empress had barely been home a few hours before he had somehow gotten himself into her room. Instantly worried the world would explode, Mom and Dad gasped at Kizmet's bold move. Empress/Not Empress was sitting on the

Jazmine's Story...by Mr. Jazz

windowsill when she saw him, and immediately issued a kitten-sized hiss, but instead of hissing back, gentle Kizmet reclined on the floor next to her with his body posture completely relaxed and non-threatening. He winked a slow blink of trust and friendship her way.

While she was still cautious, her fur flattened and she blinked back. She stopped hissing and at that very moment, Mom remembered how Kizmet stayed with me during my last hours in this room. That was when the name magically came to her.

"Jazmine," she whispered. "Kizmet, meet Jazmine."

Kizmet was there when it was time to say goodbye to me and now he was here to say hello to Jazmine, my namesake. Mom sighed contentedly and I had to agree — it *was* the perfect name: a tribute to me, and in keeping with the "z" tradition, it was spelled Jazmine rather than Jasmine. When Mom told Dad he quickly agreed and everything seemed to fall perfectly into place after that. The other boys — Rolz and Zee — welcomed her with relatively open paws. Not with as much love as Kizmet, but enough that she didn't mind them coming into her room now and again. And the girls, well, think back to the catty days of high school. That was initially Zoey, Mia, and Peanut.

"I don't think she's a real ginger," growled Zoey.

"She's such a baby," hissed Mia.

"I'm Daddy's favorite," Peanut meowed.

There was also Harley, but she spent most of her life sleeping on the couch in the living room and I don't think she even had a clue Jazmine existed.

Rescued Volume 2

Jazmine didn't seem too concerned the girls didn't like her and honestly, it was temporary anyhow. By day six of what was supposed to be a 14-day sequester, she surprised everyone by coming out of her room when Mom accidentally left the door ajar, and she joined everyone in the kitchen for dinner! She probably surprised herself the most because I don't think she was prepared to face seven pairs of startled eyes staring at her all at once!

But Jazmine was a trooper and she didn't let it faze her. From that point forward, Mom and Dad officially had a household of eight cats again. And what can I say? I know Mom and Dad loved all us kitties with every fiber of their being. But Jazmine, she was cut from the cloth of a different cat, one born of magical ginger fairy dust with a predestined mission to sprinkle her love and cheer to those that needed it most. Like me, she came from a special dimension, one that carries a unique and treasured spot in the hearts of our humans.

I was an author — dignified and reserved — born to teach my humans invaluable lessons about life, love,

Jazmine's Story...by Mr. Jazz

grieving, and letting go. My namesake is an extraordinary creature with her own lessons to teach. We both share a love of playing fetch and watching our humans from afar in the hallway, and it's startling actually, how sometimes Mom and Dad will catch sight of Jazmine and for a brief moment, they think it's me.

It's not, of course. There's only one me and there could only be one Jazmine — a ginger goddess with smoldering golden eyes, fluffy pantaloons, and a fuzzy belly that just begs to be kissed. One minute she's the Artful Dodger, craftily stealing your heart while sneaking food from your plate, the next she's a dancer swaying her luxurious and bushy tail to the beat of Gwen Stefani's *Rock Steady*. But she is my forever love gift to my humans, and for that, we will always be connected.

Ironically, Mom discovered Jazmine's story was not as it appeared. After she shared the news of Jazmine on her blog, she received an email from the woman who, with her husband, owned the farm where Jazmine was found. They were very much alive, thank you very much, and the truth was that a farmhand had been in their barn, enjoying a shrimp-topped gourmet pizza when Jazmine came out from hiding. (Jazmine could never resist a good meal.) The woman explained they already had a houseful of strays and didn't have room for another so they contacted Florida Little Dog Rescue for help. They stayed in touch with the rescue, so that's how they found Mom's blog.

The foster family also said that had Empress/Jazmine not been adopted at the expo, they would have taken her. You know how stories go, they start one way and as they're passed down, they become completely different. But honestly, the details didn't matter. Jazmine was rescued based on what Mom and Dad were told at the time, but more importantly, *and most importantly to me*, she rescued my humans and filled the empty holes in their hearts. That's all that mattered to me and I could finally rest in peace.

I came to Mom one last time after Jazmine. Precious Harley unexpectedly had to go over the Rainbow Bridge about a year after I departed and Mom was crushed. I went to the place where Harley comforted and snuggled next to me during my final days: the corner of Mom's bedroom next to the bathroom. Mom had just gotten out of the shower, and she looked down and saw me. Just as our eyes locked when I told her to go to the expo, they locked again and I reassured her with a slow blink of love that Harley was with me. It didn't make the devastating pain go away, but my visit did give her some peace, knowing Harley was not alone. I now live on in Mom and Dad's hearts through my destiny and namesake, Jazmine. And this is where I typically sign off with a peace-out to all, but I just have one more bit of magic ginger fairy dust to share with you.

When Mom was helping me write *Purr Prints*, she did something she had never done before. She went through her files to find my birth certificate and confirm exactly when she adopted me. It's not something I mention often since Mom got me as a beloved pet and not for my lineage, but I was a cat with a pedigree. She filed away my papers years ago without ever giving them a second thought.

Jazmine's Story...by Mr. Jazz

When she found my papers and pulled them out of the folder, her eyes opened wide when she saw my fur-mother's name: Jazzy Jasmine! In all my years of life, I'd never known I had the same first name as my fur-mother and neither did Mom. And the Jasmine connection — wow! Perhaps not earth-shattering news in the scheme of things, but Mom and me, we knew it was a special sign just for us.

Fate, destiny, kismet, magic...I believe. Do you?

Sparky: It's Not Over Until the Cat Lady Sings

During that terrible week last December, the hot midsummer African sun beat down mercilessly. By midday of the second day it was 86 degrees in the shade. In those final hours, I lost consciousness several times as I hovered uncertainly between life and death. It was so tempting to just let go. As I gazed up at the glorious light across The Rainbow Bridge, beckoning so beguilingly, I yearned to fly free, but the fragile silver thread still held me fast. Thin and ephemeral as it was, I could not bring myself to rip it loose from my dehydrated flesh.

As I floated dreamily above the stinking dumpster sweltering in the sun, I could see the small box taped tightly shut with my little furry white body trapped inside. The box rested on a bed of rotten potato salad

Sparky: It's Not Over...

and a discarded chicken carcass, and I feared that the flies buzzing aggressively around my coffin would finally find their way in to torment me and feast on me while I still drew breath. I imagined hordes of creamy white maggots with red eyes writhing and twisting, devouring my tender young flesh as I uttered my last, faint cry in agony. I knew then, that I had to continue the fight. I had to hold on just a little longer. Somehow deep inside, I knew this end was not my destiny. Even at that moment my spirit searched for *her*, reaching out tentatively, and the connection was made.

I was so thirsty, so hot and so hungry. The box was small, dark and stuffy and I could barely breathe as I squirmed helplessly in my own filth, yearning for the safety and comforting presence of my mother and siblings. More than anything, I wanted to be free from this torture and cuddled up safely with them, but their memory was growing dim and distant. Weakly I tried again and again to rip my way through the tough, tape-fortified walls of my cramped prison cell, but my claws were too soft to make even a scratch. I grew weaker and weaker as the hours dragged on into that second day.

That's my earliest memory. I was only a tiny kitten then, about three weeks old. I feel a little guilty sometimes because I can't remember much about my mother or my littermates. They are just a vague, warm memory that makes me a little sad and nostalgic when I think of them. I guess the ordeal affected my mind and I'm still in shock, even after almost a year. That's why I'm so attached to Gentle Hands. When people come to the house, I run away and hide under the bed or in the closet, just in case they have come to take me away from my beloved Gentle Hands. The family call her Linda, but I have my own, special name for her. I adore her and she adores me. I don't ever want to lose her like I lost my mother and siblings.

Even when Vivienne comes, I hide. Vivienne is the Good Samaritan who found me and brought me to Gentle Hands, but I still have an irrational fear that she will come one day and take me away just like the lady who came for Billy and Tommy. Gentle Hands says they are thriving and living in the lap of luxury but I don't care. I just couldn't bear to be separated from Gentle Hands now, not even to go back to Vivienne. She trusts Vivienne implicitly of course, and I know I should too, but I can only bring myself to have faith in four humans: Gentle Hands, her husband and her two daughters who helped raise me — no one else.

Vivienne unravelled the story behind the whole affair of my torture and salvation. She's a tough and tenacious old cat lady, is Vivienne. She won't rest until she gets to the bottom of a worrying situation, and then, if you're guilty, you'd better watch out! You can run and hide but in the end, Vivienne will track you down. She will spend her last breath fighting cruelty.

Vivienne eventually discovered that my mother was a feral cat living in the alley between a gas station and a grocery store. Nobody knows how she became feral. Perhaps she was abandoned to fend for herself when her uncaring humans moved away and abandoned her, like so many people do. Perhaps she was thrown

Sparky: It's Not Over...

out because she was pregnant. We can't be sure about mom's background but we do know that she was miserable and emaciated when she gave birth to me and my siblings. Vivienne is still trying to trap and sterilize her. They call her the Elusive Phantom. She has absolutely no faith in humans. Her life is a little easier now that Vivienne feeds and takes care of the colony in that alley but mom keeps evading capture and producing kittens for Vivienne to find.

The owner of the gas station where I was born was a mean and cruel man. He hated animals and cats in particular. My mother was never safe there but she had no choice. She had to live close to a ready source of food. The garbage and spoilt food from the grocery store provided her with a dubious supply of nutrition as we grew in her belly. Sometimes she was lucky enough to catch a foraging rat or mouse and get a little much-needed protein.

She slunk into the gas station's workshop one night via a broken window at the back and gave birth to us on an oily rag under a rusty old Ford pick-up that had been left to decay in the far corner of the shop. There we lived precariously, but unnoticed, for the first three weeks of my life, but as our eyes and ears began to open, we started to explore and crawled about. The mechanic discovered us one morning when my mother was out searching the dumpsters in the alley for scraps to eat. He furtively gathered us up into an old cardboard box, attempting to move us to safety before his mean boss got wind of us. Unfortunately my mother returned just as he scooped me up in his dirty hand.

Rescued Volume 2

She, understandably, had lost all faith in humans and ferociously defended us hissing, scratching and biting the well-meaning man. He dropped the box and went to tend his bleeding hands.

Mother hastily began to move us. Naturally, she could only carry us one at a time. One by one, my brothers and sisters were taken out of the workshop and hidden behind an old crate in the alley. I was the last one left. As she jumped through the window, returning to fetch me, the mean boss appeared and spotted her. He rushed at her like a raging bull. My mother and the kindly mechanic were helpless in the face of this monster. Mom fled back into the alley in terror. I was petrified by the commotion, too afraid to even try crawling to safety on my wobbly little legs. All I could do was cry pitifully.

Suddenly a rough, hard hand grabbed me by the scruff and yanked me up for inspection. He shook me so violently that I vomited up my milky breakfast all over my fur.

"You filthy, disgusting little rat! What are you vermin doing in my workshop? I'll get rid of you first and look for the rest later. There's bound to be more of you."

He spat in my face. I screamed in terror trying desperately to tear myself free from the cruel, pinching fingers that bit painfully into the delicate skin of my neck. Then he transferred me roughly to his other hand closing his fist around me in a hard, vice-like grip. I screamed, I scratched, and I kicked and bit as hard as I could. My little heart felt as if it would burst and I fought for breath but my lungs couldn't open. To this

Sparky: It's Not Over...

day I'm afraid of human hands and I don't like being picked up and held — not even by Gentle Hands.

"Please, it's only a tiny kitten..." said the mechanic as his boss grasped me in his fist.

His intervention only made matters worse. An evil grin crossed his boss's ugly face.

"No. This is too easy. It's going to be slow and painful. Bring me that empty sparkplug box. It's just the right size. Move, Dumbass! And grab that roll of tape off the workbench."

The owner forced me into the sparkplug box. Tiny as I was, I barely fit into it. I tried desperately to wriggle out of the cramped box, and the mean man hurt my leg as he forced it back in with his rough fingers. I yelped in pain, and tried unsuccessfully to bite him with my baby teeth. The man forced lid down, squashing my head into the cramped space and twisting my neck at an awkward angle. Darkness surrounded me as he wound the tape round and round the box, sealing it up tightly. The harsh, ripping sounds of the tape pulling from the roll were even more terrifying than the claustrophobia of being trapped in the box. Only a tiny crack remained in one corner which he had missed. I shoved my nose into that corner, desperately sucking in air through the minute slit.

Then came a sensation like flying as the owner tossed the box up and over the edge of the dumpster where it landed with a thud in the smelly potato salad. The jolt sent a shockwave through my body.

Throughout that first terrible day I cried and cried, trying desperately to free myself or alert someone to my plight, but nobody came. The cruel boss watched the nice mechanic like a hawk, and at the end of the day, the mechanic reluctantly went home, appalled at having to leave me there but too afraid of losing his job to defy his boss. He had a large family to support.

Nighttime brought a little relief from the suffocating heat. I cried throughout the night, hoping my mother would hear and free me but she never came. She must have been too scared to leave her other babies and come in search of me. Perhaps she did venture into the workshop to see if I was still there. I'll never know.

The mechanic also remained awake all that night. The next day, during his lunch break, he managed to slip away and tell the staff of the neighbouring grocery store about my plight. He dared not attempt a rescue effort himself — if I was still alive.

That was when my fate changed. The outraged grocery store staff climbed up into the filthy dumpster sweating as they dug around in the trash, searching for the box. By now I was no longer crying. I was teetering precariously close to death and it took them precious minutes to locate the small box.

Mercifully, they were not too late. They ripped off the tape and freed me, but by then, I was unconscious and barely breathing. Someone in the store knew about Vivienne, the crazy cat lady, who fed and cared for the ferals in the area. They called her and she immediately came racing to my rescue. She rushed me straight to the veterinarian.

I was given a shot of something to resuscitate me and several syringes of fluid directly under my dehydrated

Sparky: It's Not Over...

skin. I was too tiny for the veterinary staff to put up a drip, but in any case, my veins had all but collapsed. I was so severely dehydrated that my organs were on the brink of failure. The Rainbow Bridge, and beyond that, Planet Cat, still tantalizingly beckoned me home to an eternity free of humans and safe from the suffering they cause, but something made me resist kitty heaven a little longer. I had to find *her*.

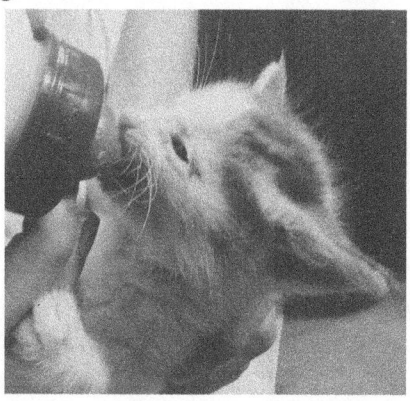

With expert veterinary care and Vivienne's kindness, I bounced back quickly, and after a night in hospital Vivienne took me home with her, unsure of what else to do. Like all the other cat ladies she knew, she was swamped with unwanted cats and kittens and had no space in her small home for yet another waif. She carried me in her handbag while she made her rounds to feed and put out water for all the feral colonies in her care. I refused to let her out of my sight and screamed blue murder every time she tried to move somewhere without me. After repeated attempts to set me down, she had no choice but to leave me clinging tenaciously to her shoulder. Every time she pulled me gently off as she drove about, I scrambled back onto her lap and clawed my way up to my safe perch just beneath her ear. She had to take me along with her even if she went out in the evening. I knew she was chosen to take me to Gentle Hands and it was only a matter of time.

Apparently I caused quite a stir, clinging to her tightly wherever she went. It was the festive season and fairy lights and candles twinkled everywhere. Someone said I sparkled like a Christmas decoration on her shoulder and the name Sparkles stuck (although my family just call me Sparky now).

This continued for a couple of days, but it really couldn't continue. Vivienne's car was hot and stuffy and I hampered her efforts to care for her ferals. She was also determined to get to the bottom of the mystery surrounding my ordeal, but with me clinging to her like a brooch and needing a feed every two or three hours, she couldn't do much. By now she had grown very attached to me and it was with some reluctance that she called Gentle Hands.

Gentle Hands had a full house, having recently taken in a litter of kittens to hand rear as well as grumpy Mewriel Purrkins (the Second), whose people were moving away and threatened to throw her out on the streets. Of course, Gentle Hands and her family took pity on Mewriel and took her in, even though she was a problem cat and they were short on room. So when Vivienne asked Gentle Hands to take me in, she should have said no. But the moment she laid eyes on me, something passed between us as we recognized each other.

Sparky: It's Not Over...

As she cradled me in her hands, lifting me up to her face to plant a kiss on my forehead, my whole being was filled with a feeling of safety and love. I realized she had been the anchor keeping my body and soul connected in that stinking dumpster. She was the reason I could not let go.

"Of course I'll take her, Viv," said Gentle Hands, and it was settled.

It was with sadness that Vivienne tiptoed quietly away, leaving me in the capable, warm hands of my new foster mother. As attached I was to Vivienne, I knew that I did not fit into her busy lifestyle of caring for hundreds of cats and campaigning against animal cruelty. I fell asleep purring, with a bottle's teat in my mouth. I thought briefly of the hard, cruel hands which had taken me from my mother, then I relaxed in these new, soft, gentle hands and I knew I'd be safe forever. Gentle Hands and her family have reared and fostered hundreds of cats like me. It wasn't the same as my mother but I was grateful to be fed, first by Vivienne and now by Gentle Hands. I never want to be hungry ever again.

Gentle Hands bottle fed me with the new litter of orphans. The vets guessed that I was about a week older than my new brothers and sister when I joined the family, and I took to them at once. Billy, Tommy, Candy and their deceased sister Mia, had started life in similar circumstances to mine. They too had been born to an abandoned mother. She had given birth to them on the premises of a used car dealership in a busy industrial area, and while she had been left in peace with her kittens by the staff, they did not think to feed her. When her kittens were two days old, the young queen went in search of food and was run over by a car. Once they were rescued, the helpless orphans were brought to Gentle Hands to be hand reared. A couple of days after their arrivial, little Mia had crossed the The Rainbow Bridge, looking for her mother. It was touch and go with Billy, Tommy and Candy for the first two weeks, but they clung to life despite the snuffles, diarrhea and ringworm they contracted. Gentle Hands and her human family soldiered on, taking turns to stay up at night and nurse the tiny feline babies who woke every two to three hours for a feed, a dose of medicine—or both.

Two of my new siblings, Billy and Tommy, found a home with a very kind lady when they were nine weeks old. Tommy was still very fragile at the time. He had never been a healthy little kitty but due to the persistence and loving care of his adopted mother, Debbie, he has turned out to be a strapping, healthy young fellow, just like Big Billy.

Sparky: It's Not Over...

Gentle Hands could not find a home suitable for Candy and me, and I suspect she didn't really want to. She's very picky about finding homes for the cats and kittens she rescues. She knows what a fraidy cat I am and she didn't have the heart to separate me from Candy or to place me with strangers. As for me, I was completely bonded with Gentle Hands and my human and feline family. With Vivienne's consent, Gentle Hands and her husband and daughters decided to keep both of us.

We are a happy family of four humans, currently twenty cats (all rescued at some point by Gentle Hands and her human family), two dogs and an icky corn snake whom I steer clear of — just in case! Medusa is harmless, they assure me, but I'm scared of her all the same. Jilly has now become my closest cat companion. I think I fill the gap left by her sister Gabby who died of FIP, a horrible disease, about two months after I came to live at the Deane residence (which they call Mewtopia). Jilly has taken me under her wing and I love my new big sister almost as much as I love Gentle Hands.

Candy and I are still close but she now prefers to hang out with Richard Parker, a new arrival who came to live with us right after summer. He's just a little older than Candy and I, and Candy thinks the world of him. He likes rough games like climbing trees and getting up on the roof. Candy is brave and adventurous like him. I prefer to stay quietly by Gentle Hands' side, resting my head on her laptop keyboard as she tries to work. I have the important job of being her chief mewse.

Rescued Volume 2

Misty has become my surrogate mommy cat. She's the boss cat here, the chief representative of Mewtopia, and the story of her rescue is even more hair-raising than mine. She is Gentle Hands' "familiar" and she graciously shares her personal human with me and Jilly. I guess we are the inner circle, sleeping on the bed between Gentle Hands and her husband at night.

On a cold, wet winter day earlier this year, Gentle Hands' husband brought KitKat to join the family. She's an old cat who lived feral for many years and she's quite a scary old dame. She smacks me off the bed sometimes when she wants a cuddle with Mr. Gentle Hands, whom she adores and regards as her own.

Callie, Silky, Felicity, Pearl, Ting-A-Ling and Smokey all prefer to hang out at the pool house at the top of the garden. They are a tight-knit sisterhood and they prefer the peacefulness up at the pool house although they sometimes come and grace us with their presence in the house. Maggie is never far from my older human sister and Noel, Tammy, Skippy and Nippy are very attached to my younger human sister. Sometimes Richard and Candy also sleep on her bed and it gets quite crowded. Mewriel Purrkins the Second is very peculiar and doesn't like anyone except Mr. Gentle Hands. She pretty much keeps to herself and won't allow anyone else into Mr. Gentle Hands' study. Pookie and Katie are best friends and hang out together on the sofas by the big French windows in the living room.

I wish I could tell you the stories behind the rescue of all my feline brothers and sisters but there isn't space for that here. This is my story. As for the dogs, well,

Sparky: It's Not Over...

they're dogs, just dogs, and they have no place in a book about cats.

But that's not quite the end of my story. Vivienne was on a mission to uncover the horrific circumstances of my rescue and would not rest until she got to the bottom of it. She bravely confronted the gas station owner and his cowed staff, and learned about my mother and her plight. Despite the owner's threats and verbal abuse, she persisted and eventually found and caught my siblings but not my mother. She placed my siblings in foster care with another cat lady just like my beloved Gentle Hands. They were eventually all homed safely with caring people. My mother has become too feral to be homed with a family, and even if Vivienne manages to catch and sterilize her, she will be released back into the alley with the other feral cats. Vivienne has added them to her long list of feral colonies which she cares for, trapping and sterilizing the adults and rescuing and homing the kittens whenever she finds them.

The garage owner now knew she was onto him, and despite his threats to kill and poison the cats, like all bullies, he backed off. You don't mess with Vivienne when she is on the warpath against animal abusers.

I'm pleased to report that the gas station changed hands recently due to relentless pressure and threat of legal action by Vivienne and others like her. The unscrupulous man sold his business and moved on. The new owner is very compassionate and sympathetic to Vivienne's cause. He not only actively supports her endeavours but helps finance the care and sterilization of the strays and feral cats like my mother, who are living behind his garage and in his workshop. His staff put out food for the cats daily, lightening Viv's load a little. Some people are cruel and unkind to cats, but it's definitely not over until the cat ladies sing.

🐾 🐾 🐾

Footnote: After this story was written, there have been a few changes at Mewtopia. Sadly, Misty lost her battle with cancer and crossed The Rainbow Bridge where she awaits us all one day along with Julie, Lulu, Picatso, Gabby and all Gentle Hands' other fur children who have gone on ahead of her. I have a new little sister and I love her to bits. She was born under similar circumstances as me. Vivienne found her wandering around in an industrial area and managed to catch her. She brought her to Gentle Hands and Jilly, Maggie and I have taken little Pan under

Sparky: It's Not Over...

our wing. She's pitch black and the family couldn't agree on a name for her. She was to be either Pango, Panther, Pandora or Pantalaimon but Pan is the name she seems to be stuck with. The other bit of good news is that Gentle Hands is going to adopt another kitty soon. Amber is a ginger feral with golden eyes. She's currently living at our veterinarian with her children but as soon as they find homes, Amber is coming to live with us. And so the story continues.

The Authors Behind the Cats

Catherine Holm (Zorro)

Catherine (aka "Cat") Holm is the award-winning author of *The Great Purr* (cat fantasy fiction) and *Driving with Cats* (memoir). She is also the author of two short story collections. Her short story "Sideways" in Volume 1 of *Rescued* received the Cat Writers' Association's prestigious President's Award. Cat loves being outside, teaching yoga, and playing with her cats. She lives in northern Vermont with her husband and six terrific cats, including rescued former feral, Zorro.

Camille May (Maxine)

Camille May is an English Writing and Women's Studies graduate from the University of Nevada, Reno. She discovered her passion for writing through the fantasy genre but has come to enjoy the craft in many forms. Her work was published in Douglas High School's first literary magazine and *The Montag*, UNR's Journal of Undergraduate Research. She spends her days writing to the tune of sassy parakeets and although she can't have cats where she lives, she's a lifelong cat person who loves spending time with Catmandu's kitties until their very own humans arrive to whisk them off to their furever homes.

Lisa Richman (Allie)

Lisa Richman's talents are many, and her career path shows it: she's a film director, author and photographer, and has won more than 50 awards in these three disciplines. Talents aside, her true passion is making emotional connections. Whether she's fashioning a poignant narrative, capturing a photo that brightens your day, or creating a film that touches your heart, she uses each medium as a way to make a genuine difference in someone's life. Lisa is also a private pilot, and the sweeping vistas she oversees inform her outlook on life. When her feet are on the ground, she is also a fearless advocate for homeless cats.

Kimberly Fleck (Wu Kitty)

Kimberly Fleck grew up on Cape Cod, MA and lived in the Boston area for many years before moving to Connecticut. She holds a BFA from the University of Massachusetts at Dartmouth and a MA in Special Education from Assumption College. She was an educator for almost fifteen years with a focus on behavior. Today she works as a social media strategist, digital photographer, artist and creative content producer. With her company Brand Fearless (www.brandfearless.com), Kimberly is committed to BRANDING her clients FEARLESSLY, helping them share their unique visions and missions with the world. She is also a long time animal advocate, wellness activist, foodie and general lover of anything that gets her creative juices flowing.

JaneA Kelley (Belladonna)

JaneA Kelley is the webmaster and chief cat slave of the award-winning cat advice blog Paws and Effect (paws-and-effect.com). She writes for Catster.com and Catster Magazine, and is the secretary and social media manager for Diabetic Cats In Need. She lives in the Pacific Northwest with her three cats, Thomas, Belladonna, and Tara.

Alisa A. Gaston-Linn (Little Pip)

Alisa A. Gaston-Linn's work has appeared in *Brain Child*, *The Sun*, *The Montreal Review*, *Hawaii Pacific Review*, *Fiction 365*, *The Faircloth Review*, *Rocky Mountain Parent*, *Black Hearts Magazine*, the anthologies *Untold Stories: Life, Love, and*  *Reproduction*, and *Creatures of Habitat*, along with other publications. She has taught creative writing to youth at Denver's Lighthouse Writers, and has volunteered as a creative writing facilitator for the Boys & Girls Club, and Urban Peak Teen Shelter. She lives in Colorado with her husband, daughter, two Weimaraners, and their most excellent rescued cat, Pippa.

The Authors Behind the Cats

Karen Nichols (Banzai)

Karen Nichols is the founder of Mousebreath Magazine (mousebreath.com) and Denmaster for the social media website Cat Scouts (catscouts.com), based on her work-in-progress book *The Cat Scout Handbook*. When she's not catering to her four rescued cats' every whim, she is a cat artist and interactive media developer. She lives in the San Francisco Bay Area with her husband (Mr. Tasty Face), and cats Tripper, Banzai, Reno, and Homer.

Marshall Bowden (Pounce)

Marshall Bowden is a freelance writer, veterinary technician, cat enabler, and spiritual seeker. He has written extensively about jazz and popular music for JazzIz, All About Jazz, and PopMatters. He compiled and edited the book *Quotable Jazz*, a unique collection of quotations by and about jazz music and musicians. Currently, he is working on a collection of short horror and dark fantasy stories and has recently published flash fiction at 101 Words. Marshall holds a BA in English Literature from Washington University and an MBA from DePaul University. He resides in Chicago.

Rescued Volume 2

Julie McAlee (Ashton)

Julie McAlee is a writer who has lived with animals her whole life. As a child, she always asked to visit the animal shelter instead of the zoo because she could take the shelter animals home. She has been rescuing animals ever since. Julie lives in Orlando with her husband and three rescued cats, who are clearly the ones in charge. She is a contributing writer to Catster and maintains her own blog, Sometimes Cats Herd You (catsherdyou.com), where you can see more of Ashton's adventures.

Karen Malena (Piggy)

Karen Malena is active in her community, encouraging new writers through local author programs and one-on-one mentoring. She's a compassionate animal lover with a biting sense of humor, which you'll find on Piggy's Facebook page.  Karen also wrote a full novel about our plucky feline heroine, called, simply, *Piggy*, which you can find on Amazon...or perhaps at one of her book signings. She also blogs true, inspirational stories at karenmalena.blogspot.com, and has written several other novels which are available on Amazon.

The Authors Behind the Cats

Deborah Barnes (Mr. Jazz and Jazmine)

Deborah Barnes is the author of *Makin' Biscuits — Weird Cat Habits and the Even Weirder Habits of the Humans Who Love Them*; *Purr Prints of the Heart — A Cat's Tale of Life, Death, and Beyond;* and *The Chronicles of Zee & Zoey — A Journey of the Extraordinarily Ordinary,* as well as the award-winning blog, *Zee & Zoey's Cat Chronicles* (zeezoey.com). She is vice president of the Cat Writers' Association and secretary of the nonprofit, Pawsitively Humane, Inc. of Miami, Florida. Her freelance work has been featured in *Cat Fancy* magazine, *Kittens 101*, Catster.com, BlogPaws.com, TheCatSite.com, and the *American Association of Human-Animal Bond Veterinarians* newsletter.

Linda Deane (Sparky)

Linda Deane is an avid cat fan. She hails from South Africa but now lives in Wellington, New Zealand with her husband and cats. She is an active member of the online animal rescue and rehome community, taking in abandoned  cats and kittens as a foster "parent" until good homes can be found for them. Her close relationship with cats has taught her much about their ways and her love for them has inspired her writing. She is never short of a "mewse" or two, or three, or four....

About the Editor

Janiss Garza is the founder of FitCat Publishing. She began her writing and editing career in the late 1980s as a music journalist, specializing in alternative rock and heavy metal. In 1989, she became senior editor at legendary rock magazine, *RIP*, a position she held for 7 years. Her writing credits include the *Los Angeles Times*, *L.A. Weekly*, *Entertainment Weekly*, the Allmovie Guide online, Yahoo Music, *Cat Fancy*, Catster.com, CatChannel.com, and the award-winning blog, Sparkle-cat.com. Janiss is the co-author of *White Line Fever* with Motörhead frontman and heavy metal icon Lemmy Kilmister, and ghostwriter for Sparkle the Designer Cat's two books, *Dear Sparkle: Advice From One Cat to Another* and *Dear Sparkle: Cat-to-Cat Advice From the World's Foremost Feline Columnist*. She created FitCat to combine a traditional publishing approach with the personal touch of an indie publisher.

Janiss is also a photographer, and volunteers for a therapy pet organization with her cat, Summer.

www.ingramcontent.com/pod-product-compliance
Lightning Source LLC
LaVergne TN
LVHW091251080426
835510LV00007B/207